Daniel Garrison Brinton

The religious sentiment, its source and aim; a contribution to the science and philosophy of religion

Daniel Garrison Brinton

The religious sentiment, its source and aim; a contribution to the science and philosophy of religion

ISBN/EAN: 9783337261634

Printed in Europe, USA, Canada, Australia, Japan

Cover: Foto ©Lupo / pixelio.de

More available books at **www.hansebooks.com**

THE
RELIGIOUS SENTIMENT

ITS SOURCE AND AIM

A CONTRIBUTION TO THE SCIENCE AND PHILOSOPHY OF RELIGION.

BY

DANIEL G. BRINTON, A.M., M.D.

Member of the American Philosophical Society, the American Philological Society, etc.; author of "The Myths of the New World," etc.

NEW YORK
HENRY HOLT AND COMPANY
1876.

COPYRIGHT,
BY HENRY HOLT,
1876.

JOHN F. TROW & SON, PRINTERS,
205-213 EAST 12TH ST., NEW YORK.

PREFACE.

MYTHOLOGY, since it began to receive a scientific handling at all, has been treated as a subordinate branch of history or of ethnology. The "science of religion," as we know it in the works of Burnouf, Müller, and others, is a comparison of systems of worship in their historic development. The deeper inquiry as to what in the mind of man gave birth to religion in any of its forms, what spirit breathed and is ever breathing life into these dry bones, this, the final and highest question of all, has had but passing or prejudiced attention. To its investigation this book is devoted.

The analysis of the religious sentiment I offer is an inductive one, whose outlines were furnished by a preliminary study of the religions of the native race of America, a field selected as most favorable by reason of the simplicity of many of its cults, and the absence of theories respecting them. This study was embodied in "The Myths of the New World; a Treatise on the Symbolism and Mythology of the Red Race of America" (second edition, N. Y. 1876).

The results thus obtained I have in the present work expanded by including in the survey the historic religions of the Old World, and submitted the whole for solution to the Laws of Mind, regarded as physiological elements of growth, and to the Laws of Thought, these, as formal only, being held as nowise a development of those. This latter position, which is not conceded by the reigning school of psychology, I have taken pains to explain and defend as far as consistent with the plan of this treatise; but I am well aware that to say all that can be said in proof of it, would take much more space than here allowed.

The main questions I have had before me in writing this volume have an interest beyond those which mere science propounds. What led men to imagine gods at all? What still prompts enlightened nations to worship? Is prayer of any avail, or of none? Is faith the last ground of adoration, or is reason? Is religion a transient phase of development, or is it the chief end of man? What is its warrant of continuance? If it overlive this day of crumbling theologies, whence will come its reprieve?

To such inquiries as these, answers satisfactory to thinking men of this time can, I believe, be given only by an inductive study of religions, supported by a sound psychology, and conducted in a spirit which acknowledges as possibly rightful, the reverence which every system claims. Those I propose, inadequate though they may be, can at any rate pretend to be the result of honest labor.

PHILADELPHIA, *January*, 1876.

CONTENTS.

CHAPTER I.
                                                                PAGE.
THE BEARING OF THE LAWS OF MIND ON RELIGION..   3

CHAPTER II.
THE EMOTIONAL ELEMENTS OF THE RELIGIOUS SENTIMENT......................................   47

CHAPTER III.
THE RATIONAL POSTULATES OF THE RELIGIOUS SENTIMENT......................................   87

CHAPTER IV.
THE PRAYER AND ITS ANSWER....................   117

CHAPTER V.
THE MYTH AND THE MYTHICAL CYCLES.............   155

CHAPTER VI.
THE CULT, ITS SYMBOLS AND RITES...............   199

CHAPTER VII.
THE MOMENTA OF RELIGIOUS THOUGHT.............   231

THE BEARING OF THE LAWS OF MIND ON RELIGION

SUMMARY.

The distinction between the Science and the Philosophy of religion. It is assumed (1) that religions are products of thought, (2) that they have a unity of kind and purpose. They can be studied by the methods of natural science applied to Mind.

Mind is co-extensive with organism. Sensation and Emotion are prominent marks of it. These are either pleasurable or painful; the latter *diminish* vital motions, the former *increase* them. This is a product of natural selection. A mis-reading of these facts is the fallacy of Buddhism and other pessimistic systems. Pleasure comes from continuous action. This is illustrated by the esthetic emotions, volition and consciousness.

The climax of mind is Intellect. Physical changes accompany thought but cannot measure it. Relations of thought and feeling. *Truth* is its only measure. Truth, like pleasure, is desired for its preservative powers. It is reached through the laws of thought.

These laws are : (1) the natural order of the association of ideas, (2) the methods of applied logic, (3) the forms of correct reasoning. The last allow of mathematical expression. They are three in number, called those of Determination, Limitation and Excluded Middle.

The last is the key-stone of religious philosophy. Its diverse interpretations. Its mathematical expression shows that it does not relate to contradictories. But certain concrete analytic propositions, relating to contraries, do have this form. The contrary as distinguished from the privative. The Conditioned and Unconditioned, the Knowable and Unknowable are not true contradictions. The synthesis of contraries is theoretic only.

Errors as to the limits of possible explanation corrected by these distinctions. The formal law is the last and complete explanation. The relations of thought, belief and being.

THE RELIGIOUS SENTIMENT.

CHAPTER I.

THE BEARING OF THE LAWS OF MIND ON RELIGION.

The Science of Religion is one of the branches of general historical science. It embraces, as the domain of its investigation, all recorded facts relating to the displays of the Religious Sentiment. Its limits are defined by those facts, and the legitimate inferences from them. Its aim is to ascertain the constitutive laws of the origin and spread of religions, and to depict the influence they have exerted on the general life of mankind.

The question whether a given religion is true or false cannot present itself in this form as a proper subject of scientific inquiry. The most that can be asked is, whether some one system is best suited to a specified condition of the individual or the community.

The higher inquiry is the object of the

Philosophy of Religion. This branch of study aims to pass beyond recorded facts and local adjustments in order to weigh the theoretical claims of religions, and measure their greater or less conformity with abstract truth. The formal or regulative laws of religious thought occupy it.

Theology, dogmatic or polemic, is an explanatory defence of some particular faith. Together with mythology and symbolism, it furnishes the material from which the Science and Philosophy of Religion seek to educe the laws and frame the generalizations which will explain the source and aim of religion in general.

The common source of all devotional displays is the Religious Sentiment, a complex feeling, a thorough understanding of which is an essential preliminary to the study of religious systems.

Such a study proceeds on the assumption that all religions are products of thought, commenced and continued in accordance with the laws of the human mind, and, therefore, comprehensible to the extent to which these laws are known. No one disputes this, except in reference to his own religion. This, he is apt to assert, had something "supernatural" about its origin. If this word be correctly used, it may stand without cavil. The "natural" is that of which we know in whole or in part the laws; the "supernatural" means that of which we do not at present know in any degree the laws. The domain of the supernatural diminishes in the ratio of the increase of knowledge; and the inference that it also is absolutely under the control of law, is not only allowable but obligatory.

A second assumption must be that there is a unity of kind and purpose in all religions. Without this, no common law can exist for them. Such a law must hold good in all ages, in every condition of society, and in each instance. Hence those who explain religious systems as forms of government, or as systems of ethics, or as misconceived history, or as theories of natural philosophy, must be prepared to make their view good when it is universally applied, or else renounce the possibility of a Science of Religion; while those who would except their own system from what they grant is the law of all others, violate the principles of investigation and thereby the canons of truth.

The methods of science are everywhere alike. Has the naturalist to explain an organism, he begins with its elements or proximate principles as obtained by analysis; he thence passes to the tissues and fluids which compose its members; these he considers first in a state of repose, their structure and their connections; then he examines their functions, the laws of their growth and action; and finally he has recourse to the doctrine of relations, *la théorie des milieux*, to define the conditions of its existence. Were such a method applied to a religion, it would lead us first to study its psychological elements, then the various expressions in word and act to which these give occasion, next the record of its growth and decay, and finally from these to gather the circumstantials of human life and culture which led to its historic existence.

Some have urged that such a method should not be summoned to questions in mental philosophy. To do so, say they, is to confound things distinct, requiring distinct plans of study. Such a criticism might have had weight in the days when the mind was supposed to inhabit the body as a tenant a house, and have no relation to it other than that of a casual occupant. But that opinion is antiquated. More than three-fourths of a century ago the far-seeing thinker, Wilhelm von Humboldt, laid down the maxim that the phenomena of mind and matter obey laws identical in kind;[1] and a recent historian of science sums up the result of the latest research in these words:

"The old dualism of mind and body, which for centuries struggled in vain for reconciliation, finds it now, not indeed in the unity of substance, but in the unity of laws."[2]

[1] In his essay entitled, *Ueber den Geschlechtsunterschied und dessen Einfluss auf die organische Natur*, first published in 1795.
[2] "Der alte Dualismus von Geist und Körper, der Jahrhun-

It is, therefore, as a question in mental philosophy to be treated by the methods of natural science, that I shall approach the discussion of the religious sentiment. As it is a part, or at least a manifestation of mind, I must preface its more particular consideration with some words on the mind in general, words which I shall make as few and as clear as possible.

At the beginning of this century, the naturalist Oken hazarded the assertion: "The human mind is a memberment of infusorial sensation,"[1] a phrase which has been the guiding principle of scientific psychology ever since. That in the course of this memberment or growth wholly new faculties are acquired, is conceded. As the union of two inorganic substances may yield a third different in every respect from either; or, as in the transition of inorganic to organic matter, the power of reproduction is attained; so, positively new powers may attend the development of mind. From sensations it progresses to emotions, from emotions to reason. The one is the psychical climax of the other. "We have still to do with the one mind, whose action devel-

---

derte hindurch nach Versöhnung gerungen, findet diese heute nicht zwar in der Einheit der Substanz, wohl aber in der Einheit des Gesetzes." Dr. Heinrich Boehmer, *Geschichte der Entwickelung der Naturwissenschaftlichen Weltanschauung in Deutschland*, s. 201 (Gotha, 1872).

[1] *Elements of Physio-Philosophy*, § 3589. Eng. trans., London, 1847.

opes itself with perception, through discrimination, till it arrives at notions, wherein its most general scheme, 'truth and error,' serves as the principle."[1]

Extravagant as Oken's expression seemed to many when it was published, it now falls short of the legitimate demands of science, and I may add, of religion. *Mind is co-extensive with organism;* in the language of logic, one "connotes" the other; this statement, and nothing short of it, satisfies the conditions of the problem. Wherever we see Form preserved amid the change of substance, *there* is mind; it alone can work that miracle; only it gives Life. Matter suffers no increase; therefore the new is but a redistribution of the old; it is new in *form* only; and the maintenance of form under changes of substance is the one distinguishing mark of organism. To it is added the yet more wonderful power of transmitting form by reproduction. Wherever these are, are also the rudiments of mind. The distinction between the animal and the vegetable worlds, between the reasoning and unreasoning animals, is one of degree only. Whether, in a somewhat different sense, we should not go yet further, and say that mind is co-extensive with motion, and hence with phenomena, is a speculative inquiry which may have to be

---

[1] Von Feuchtersleben, *The Principles of Medical Psychology*, p. 130 (Eng. trans., London, 1847).

answered in the affirmative, but it does not concern us here.

The first and most general mark of Mind is sensation or common feeling. In technical language a sensation is defined to be the result of an impression on an organism, producing some molecular change in its nerve or life centres. It is the consequence of a contact with another existence. Measured by its effects upon the individual the common law of sensation is: Every impression, however slight, either adds to or takes from the sum of the life-force of the system; in the former case it produces a pleasurable, in the latter a painful sensation. The exceptions to this rule, though many, are such in appearance only.[1]

In the human race the impression can often be made quite as forcibly by a thought as by an act. "I am confident," says John Hunter, the anatomist, "that I can fix my attention to any

---

[1] "The fundamental property of organic structure is to seek what is beneficial, and to shun what is hurtful to it." Dr. Henry Maudsley, *Body and Mind*, p. 22.

"The most essential nature of a sentient being is to move *to* pleasure and *from* pain." A. Bain, *On the Study of Character*, p. 292 (London, 1861).

"States of Pleasure are connected with an increase, states of Pain with an abatement of some or all of the vital functions." A. Bain, *Mind and Body*, p. 59.

"Affectus est confusa idea, quâ Mens majorem, vel minorem sui corporis, vel alicujus ejus partis, existendi vim affirmat." Spinoza, *Ethices*, Lib. III. *ad finem*.

part, until I have a sensation in that part." This is what is called the influence of the mind upon the body. Its extent is much greater than used to be imagined, and it has been a fertile source of religious delusions. Such sensations are called subjective; those produced by external force, objective.

The immediate consequent of a sensation is *reflex action*, the object of which is either to avoid pain or increase pleasure, in other words, either to preserve or augment the individual life.

The molecular changes incident to a sensation leave permanent traces, which are the physical bases of memory. One or several such remembered sensations, evoked by a present sensation, combine with it to form an Emotion. Characteristic of their origin is it that the emotions fall naturally into a dual classification, in which the one involves pleasurable or elevating, the other painful or depressing conditions. Thus we have the pairs joy and grief, hope and fear, love and hate, etc.

The question of pleasure and pain is thus seen to be the primary one of mental science. We must look to it to explain the meaning of sensation as a common quality of organism. What is the significance of pleasure and pain?

The question involves that of Life. Not to stray into foreign topics, it may broadly be said that as all change resolves itself into motion, and, as Helmholtz remarks, all science merges itself into mechanics, we should commence by asking what vital motions these sensations stand for or correspond to.

Every organism, and each of its parts, is the resultant of innumerable motions, a composition of forces. As such, each obeys the first law of motion, to wit, indefinite continuance of action until interfered with. This is a modification of Newton's "law of continuance," which, with the other primary laws of motion, must be taken as the foundation of biology as well as of astronomy.[1]

The diminution or dispersion of organic motion is expressed in physiological terms as *waste;* we are admonished of waste by *pain;* and thus admonished we supply the waste or avoid the injury as far as we can. But this connection of pain with waste is not a necessary one, nor is it the work of a *Providentia particularis,* as the

---

[1] The extension of the mechanical laws of motion to organic motion was, I believe, first carried out by Comte. His biological form of the first law is as follows: "Tout état, statique ou dynamique, tend à persister spontanément, sans aucune altération, en resistant aux perturbations extérieures." *Système de Politique Positive,* Tome iv. p. 178. The metaphysical ground of this law has, I think, been very well shown by Schopenhauer to be in the Kantian principle that time is not a force, nor a quality of matter, but a condition of perception, and hence it can exert no physical influence. See Schopenhauer, *Parerga und Paralipomena,* Bd. II, s. 37.

schoolmen said. It is a simple result of natural selection. Many organisms have been born, no doubt, in which waste did not cause pain; caused, perhaps, pleasure. Consequently, they indulged their preferences and soon perished. Only those lived to propagate their kind in whom a different sensation was associated with waste, and they transmitted this sensitiveness increased by ancestral impression to their offspring. The curses of the human race to-day are alcohol, opium and tobacco, and they are so because they cause waste, but do not immediately produce painful but rather pleasurable feelings.

Pain, as the sensation of waste, is the precursor of death, of the part or system. By parity of evolution, pleasure came to be the sensation of continuance, of uninterrupted action, of increasing vigor and life. Every action, however, is accompanied by waste, and hence every pleasure developes pain. But it is all important to note that the latter is the mental correlative not of the action but of its cessation, not of the life of the part but of its ceasing to live. Pain, it is true, in certain limits excites to action; but it is by awakening the self-preservative tendencies, which are the real actors. This physiological distinction, capable of illustration from sensitive vegetable as well as the lowest animal organisms, has had an intimate connection with religious theories. The problems of suffering and death are precisely the ones which all religions set forth to solve in theory and in practice. Their creeds and myths are based on what they make of pain. The theory of Buddhism, which now has more followers than any other faith, is founded on four axioms, which are called "the four excellent truths." The first and fundamental one is: "Pain is inseparable from existence." This is the principle of all pessimism, ancient and modern. Schopenhauer, an out-and-out pessimist, lays down the allied maxim, "All pleasure is negative, that is, it consists in getting rid of a want or pain,"[1] a principle expressed before his time in the saying "the highest pleasure is the relief from pain."

Consistently with this, Buddhism holds out as the ultimate of hope the state of Nirvana, in which existence is not, where the soul is "blown out" like the flame of a candle.

But physiology demolishes the corner-stone of this edifice when it shows that pain, so far from being inseparable from existence, has merely become, through transmitted experience, nearly inseparable from the progressive cessation of existence. While action and reaction are equal in inorganic nature, the principle of life modifies the operation of this universal law of force by

[1] "Aller Genuss, seiner Natur nach, ist negativ, d. h., in Befreiung von einer Noth oder Pein besteht." *Parerga und Paralipomena.* Bd. II. s. 482.

bringing in *nutrition,* which, were it complete, would antagonize reaction. In such a case, pleasure would be continuous, pain null; action constant, reaction hypothetical. As, however, nutrition in fact never wholly and at once replaces the elements altered by vital action, both physicians and metaphysicians have observed that pleasure is the fore-runner of pain, and has the latter as its certain sequel.[1]

Physiologically and practically, the definition of pleasure is, *maximum action with minimum waste.*

This latter generalization is the explanation of the esthetic emotions. The modern theory of art rests not on a psychological but a physiological, and this in turn on a physical basis. Helmholtz's theory of musical harmony depends on the experimental fact that a continued impression gives a pleasant, a discontinuous an unpleasant sensation. The mechanics of muscular structure prove that what are called graceful motions are

---

[1] "No impression whatever is pleasant beyond the instant of its realization; since, at that very instant, commences the change of susceptibility, which suggests the desire for a change of impression or for a renewal of that impression which is fading away." Dr. J. P. Catlow, *The Principles of Aesthetic Medicine,* p 155 (London, 1867).

"Dum re, quem appetamus fruimur, corpus ex ea fruitione novam acquirat constitutionem, á quá aliter determinatur, et aliæ rerum imagines in eo excitantur," etc. Spinoza, *Ethices,* Pars III, Prop. lix.

those which are the mechanical resultant of the force of the muscle,—those which it can perform at least waste. The pleasure we take in curves, especially "the line of beauty," is because our eyes can follow them with a minimum action of its muscles of attachment. The popular figure called the Grecian figure or the walls of Troy, is pleasant because each straight line is shorter, and at right angles to the preceding one, thus giving the greatest possible change of action to the muscles of the eye.

Such a mechanical view of physiology presents other suggestions. The laws of vibratory motion lead to the inference that action in accordance with those laws gives maximum intensity and minimum waste. Hence the pleasure the mind takes in harmonies of sound, of color and of odors.

The correct physiological conception of the most perfect physical life is that which will continue the longest in use, not that which can display the greatest muscular force. The ideal is one of extension, not of intension.

Religious art indicates the gradual recognition of these principles. True to their ideal of inaction, the Oriental nations represent their gods as mighty in stature, with prominent muscles, but sitting or reclining, often with closed eyes or folded hands, wrapped in robes, and lost in meditation. The Greeks, on the other hand, portrayed their deities of ordinary stature, naked, awake and erect, but the limbs smooth and round, the muscular lines and the veins hardly visible, so that in every attitude an indefinite sense of repose pervades the whole figure. Movement without effort, action without waste, is the immortality these incomparable works set forth. They are meant to teach that the ideal life is one, not of painless ease, but of joyous action.

The law of continuity to which I have alluded is not confined to simple motions. It is a general mathematical law, that the longer anything lasts the longer it is likely to last. If a die turns ace a dozen times handrunning, the chances are large that it will turn ace again. The Theory of Probabilities is founded upon this, and the value of statistics is based on an allied principle. Every condition opposes change through inertia. By this law, as the motion caused by a pleasurable sensation excites by the physical laws of associated motions the reminiscences of former pleasures and pains, a tendency to permanence is acquired, which gives the physical basis for Volition. Experience and memory are, therefore, necessary to volition, and practically self restraint is secured by calling numerous past sensations to mind, deterrent ones, "the pains which are indirect pleasures," or else pleasurable ones.

The Will is an exhibition under complex relations of the tendency to continuance which is expressed in the first law of motion. Its normal action is the maintenance of the individual life, the prolongation of the pleasurable sensations, the support of the forces which combat death.

Whatever the action, whether conscious or reflex, its real though often indirect and unaccomplished object is the preservation or the augmentation of the individual life. Such is the dictum of natural science, and it coincides singularly with the famous maxim of Spinoza: *Unaquaeque res, quantum in se est, in suo esse perseverare conatur.*

The consciousness which accompanies volitional action is derived from the common feeling which an organism has, as the result of all its parts deriving their nutrition from the same centre. Rising into the sphere of emotions, this at first muscular sensation becomes "self-feeling." The Individual is another name for the boundaries of reflex action.

Through memory and consciousness we reach that function of the mind called the intellect or reason, the product of which is *thought*. Its physical accompaniments are chemical action, and an increase of temperature in the brain. But the sum of the physical forces thus evolved is not the measure of the results of intellectual action. These differ from other forms of force in being incommensurate with extension. They cannot be appraised in units of quantity, but in quality only. The chemico-vital forces by which a thought rises into consciousness bear not the slightest relation to the value of the thought itself. It is here as in those ancient myths where an earthly maiden brings forth a god. The power of the thought is dependent on another test than physical force, to wit, its *truth*. This is measured by its conformity to the laws of right reasoning, laws clearly ascertained, which are the common basis of all science, and to which it is the special province of the science of logic to give formal expression.

Physical force itself, in whatever form it appears, is only known to us as feeling or as thought; these alone we know to be real; all else is at least less real.[1] Not only is this true of the external world, but also of that assumed something, the reason, the soul, the ego, or the intellect. For the sake of convenience these words may be used; but it is well to know that

---

[1] "Feeling and thought are much more real than anything else; they are the only things which we directly know to be real." —John Stuart Mill.—*Theism*, p. 202. How very remote external objects are from what we take them to be, is constantly shown in physiological studies. As Helmholtz remarks: "No kind and no degree of similarity exists between the quality of a sensation, and the quality of the agent inducing it and portrayed by it."—*Lectures on Scientific Subjects*, p. 390.

this introduction of something that thinks, back of thought itself, is a mere figure of speech. We say, "*I* think," as if the "I" was something else than the thinking. At most, it is but the relation of the thoughts. Pushed further, it becomes the limitation of thought by sensation, the higher by the lower. The Cartesian maxim, *cogito ergo sum*, has perpetuated this error, and the modern philosophy of the *ego* and *non-ego* has prevented its detection. A false reading of self-consciousness led to this assumption of "a thinking mind." Our personality is but the perception of the solidarity of our thoughts and feelings; it is itself a thought.

These three manifestations of mind—sensations, emotions and thoughts—are mutually exclusive in their tendencies. The patient forgets the fear of the result in the pain of the operation; in intense thought the pulse falls, the senses do not respond, emotions and action are absent. We may say that ideally the unimpeded exercise of the intellect forbids either sensation or emotion.

Contrasting sensation and emotion, on the one side, with intellect on the other, feeling with thought, they are seen to be polar or antithetical manifestations of mind. Each requires the other for its existence, yet in such wise that the one is developed at the expense of the other. The one waxes as the other wanes. This is seen to advantage when their most similar elements are compared. Thus consciousness in sensation is keenest when impressions are strongest; but this consciousness is a bar to intellectual self-consciousness, as was pointed out by Professor Ferrier in his general Law of consciousness.[1] When emotion and sensation are at their minimum, one is most conscious of the solidarity of one's thoughts; and just in proportion to the vividness of self-consciousness is thought lucid and strong. In an ideal intelligence, self-consciousness would be infinite, sensation infinitesimal.

Yet there is a parallelism between feeling and thought, as well as a contrast. As pain and pleasure indicate opposite tendencies in the forces which guide sensation and emotion, so do the true and the untrue direct thought, and bear the same relation to it. For as pain is the warning of death, so the untrue is the detrimental, the destructive. The man who reasons falsely, will act unwisely and run into danger thereby. To know the truth is to be ready for the worst. Who reasons correctly will live the longest. To love pleasure is not more in the grain of man than to desire truth. "I have known many," says St. Augustine, "who like to deceive; to be deceived, none." Pleasure, joy, truth, are the respective measures of life in sensation, emotion, intellect; one or the other of these every organ-

[1] *The Philosophy of Consciousness*, p. 72.

ism seeks with all its might, its choice depending on which of these divisions of mind is prominently its own. As the last mentioned is the climax, truth presents itself as in some way the perfect expression of life.

We have seen what pleasure is, but what is truth? The question of Pilate remains, not indeed unanswered, but answered vaguely and discrepantly.[1] We may pass it by as one of speculative interest merely, and turn our attention to its practical paraphrase, what is true?

The rules of evidence as regards events are well known, and also the principles of reaching the laws of phenomena by inductive methods. Many say that the mind can go no further than this, that the truth thus reached, if not the highest, is at least the highest for man. It is at best relative, but it is real. The correctness of this statement may be tested by analyzing the processes by which we acquire knowledge.

Knowledge reaches the mind in two forms, for which there are in most languages, though not in

---

[1] The Gospel of John (ch. xviii.) leaves the impression that Pilate either did not wait for an answer but asked the question in contempt, as Bacon understood, or else that waiting he received no answer. The Gospel of Nicodemus, however, written according to Tischendorf in the second century, probably from tradition, gives the rest of the conversation as follows: "Pilate says to him: What is truth? Jesus says: Truth is from heaven. Pilate says: Is not there truth upon earth? Jesus says to Pilate: See how one who speaks truth is judged by those who have power upon earth'" [ch. iii.]

modern English, two distinct expressions, *connaitre* and *savoir*, *kennen* and *wissen*. The former relates to knowledge through sensation, the latter through intellection; the former cannot be rendered in words, the latter can be; the former is reached through immediate perception, the latter through logical processes. For example: an odor is something we may certainly know and can identify, but we cannot possibly describe it in words; justice on the other hand may be clearly defined to our mind, but it is equally impossible to translate it into sensation. Nevertheless, it is generally agreed that the one of these processes is, so far as it goes, as conclusive as the other, and that they proceed on essentially the same principles.[1] Religious philosophy has to do only with the second form of knowledge, that reached through notions or thoughts.

The enchainment or sequence of thoughts in the mind is at first an accidental one. They arise through the two general relations of nearness in time or similarity in sensation. Their succession is prescribed by these conditions, and without conscious effort cannot be changed. They are notions about phenomena only, and hence are infinitely more likely to be wrong

---

[1] The most acute recent discussion of this subject is by Helmholtz, in his essay entitled, "*Recent Progress in the Theory of Vision.*"

than right. Of the innumerable associations of thought possible, only one can yield the truth. The beneficial effects of this one were felt, and thus by experience man slowly came to distinguish the true as what is good for him, the untrue as what is injurious.

After he had done this for a while, he attempted to find out some plan in accordance with which he could so arrange his thoughts that they should always produce this desirable result. He was thus led to establish the rules for right reasoning, which are now familiarly known as Logic. This science was long looked upon as a completed one, and at the commencement of this century we find such a thinker as Coleridge expressing an opinion that further development in it was not to be expected. Since then it has, however, taken a fresh start, and by its growth has laid the foundation for a system of metaphysics which will be free from the vagaries and unrealities which have thrown general discredit on the name of philosophy.

In one direction, as applied logic and the logic of induction, the natural associations of ideas have been thoroughly studied, and the methods by which they can be controlled and reduced have been taught with eminent success. In this branch, Bentham, Mill, Bain, and others have been prominent workers.

Dealing mainly with the subjects and materials

of reasoning, with thoughts rather than with thinking, these writers, with the tendency of specialists, have not appreciated the labors of another school of logicians, who have made the investigation of the process of thinking itself their especial province. This is abstract logic, or pure logic, sometimes called, inasmuch as it deals with forms only, "formal logic," or because it deals with names and not things, "the logic of names." It dates its rise as an independent science from the discovery of what is known as "the quantification of the predicate," claimed by Sir William Hamilton. Of writers upon it may be mentioned Professor De Morgan, W. Stanley Jevons, and especially Professor George Boole of Belfast. The latter, one of the subtlest thinkers of this age, and eminent as a mathematician, succeeded in making an ultimate analysis of the laws of thinking, and in giving them a symbolic notation, by which not only the truth of a simple proposition but the relative degree of truth in complex propositions may be accurately estimated.[1]

---

[1] George Boole, Professor of Mathematics in Queen's College, Cork, was born Nov. 2, 1815, died Dec. 8, 1864. He was the author of several contributions to the higher mathematics, but his principal production is entitled: *An Investigation into the Laws of Thought, on which are founded the mathematical Theories of Logic and Probabilities* [London, 1854.] Though the reputation he gained was so limited that one may seek his name in vain in the *New American Cyclopedia* [1875], or the *Diction-*

This he did by showing that the laws of correct thinking can be expressed in algebraic notation, and, thus expressed, will be subject to all the mathematical laws of an algebra whose symbols bear the uniform value of unity or nought (1 or 0)—a limitation required by the fact that pure logic deals in notions of quality only, not of quantity.

This mathematical form of logic was foreseen by Kant when he declared that all mathematical reasoning derives its validity from the logical laws; but no one before Professor Boole had succeeded in reaching the notation which subordinated these two divisions of abstract thought to the same formal types. His labors have not yet borne fruit in proportion to their value, and they are, I believe, comparatively little known. But in the future they will be regarded as epochal in the science of mind. They make us to see the same law governing mind and matter, thought and extension.

Not the least important result thus achieved

---

naire des Contemporains [1859]. the few who can appreciate his treatise place the very highest estimate upon it. Professor Todhunter, in the preface to his *History of the Theory of Probabilities*, calls it "a marvellous work," and in similar language Professor W. Stanley Jevons speaks of it as "one of the most marvellous and admirable pieces of reasoning ever put together" (*Pure Logic*, p. 75). Professor Bain, who gives a synopsis of it in his *Deductive Logic*, wholly misapprehends the author's purpose, and is unable to appraise justly his conclusions.

was in emphasizing the contrast between the natural laws of mental association, and the laws of thinking which are the foundation of the syllogism.

By attending to this distinction we are enabled to keep the form and the matter of thought well apart—a neglect to do which, or rather a studied attempt to ignore which, is the radical error of the logic devised by Hegel, as I shall show more fully a little later.

All applied logic, inductive as well as deductive, is based on formal logic, and this in turn on the "laws of thought," or rather of thinking. These are strictly regulative or abstract, and differ altogether from the natural laws of thought, such as those of similarity, contiguity and harmony, as well as from the rules of applied logic, such as those of agreement and difference. The fundamental laws of thinking are three in number, and their bearing on all the higher questions of religious philosophy is so immediate that their consideration becomes of the last moment in such a study as this. They are called the laws of Determination, Limitation and Excluded Middle.

The first affirms that every object thought about must be conceived as itself, and not as some other thing. "A is A," or "$x = x$," is its formal expression. This teaches us that whatever we think of, must be thought as one or a unity. It is important, however, to note that this does not mean a mathematical unit, but a logical one, that is, identity and not contrast. So true is this that in mathematical logic the only value which can satisfy the formula is a concept which does not admit of increase, to wit, a Universal.

From this necessity of conceiving a thought under unity has arisen the interesting tendency, so frequently observable even in early times, to speak of the universe as one whole, the τὸ πᾶν of the Greek philosophers; and also the monotheistic leaning of all thinkers, no matter what their creed, who have attained very general conceptions. Furthermore, the strong liability of confounding this speculative or logical unity with the concrete notion of individuality, or mathematical unity, has been, as I shall show hereafter, a fruitful source of error in both religious and metaphysical theories. Pure logic deals with quality only, not with quantity.

The second law is that of Limitation. As the first is sometimes called that of Affirmation, so this is called that of Negation. It prescribes that a thing is not that which it is not. Its formula is, "A is not not-A." If this seems trivial, it is because it is so familiar.

These two laws are two aspects of the same law. The old maxim is, *omnis determinatio est negatio;* a quality can rise into cognition only by being limited by that which it is not.

It is not a comparison of two thoughts, however, nor does it limit the quality itself. For the negative is not a thought, and the quality is not *in suo genere finita,* to use an expression of the old logicians; it is limited not by itself but by that which it is not. These are not idle distinctions, as will soon appear.

The third law comes into play when two thoughts are associated and compared. There is qualitative identity, or there is not. A is either B or not B. An animal is either a man or not a man. There is no middle class between the two to which it can be assigned. Superficial truism as this appears, we have now come upon the very battle ground of the philosophies. This is the famous " Law of the contradictories and excluded middle," on the construction of which the whole fabric of religious dogma, and I may add of the higher metaphysics, must depend. " One of the principal retarding causes of philosophy," remarks Professor Ferrier, " has been the want of a clear and developed doctrine of the contradictory." [1] The want is as old as the days of Heraclitus of Ephesus, and lent to his subtle paradoxes that obscurity which has not yet been wholly removed.

Founding his arguments on one construction of this law, expressed in the maxim, "The con-

---

[1] *The Institutes of Metaphysic*, p. 459, (2nd edition.)

ceivable lies between two contradictory extremes," Sir William Hamilton defended with his wide learning those theories of the Conditioned and the Unconditioned, the Knowable and Unknowable, which banish religion from the realm of reason and knowledge to that of faith, and cleave an impassable chasm between the human and the divine intelligence. From this unfavorable ground his orthodox followers, Mansel and Mozley, defended with ability but poor success their Christianity against Herbert Spencer and his disciples, who also accepted the same theories, but followed them out to their legitimate conclusion—a substantially atheistic one.

Hamilton in this was himself but a follower of Kant, who brought this law to support his celebrated "antinomies of the human understanding," warnings set up to all metaphysical explorers to keep off of holy ground.

On another construction of it, one which sought to escape the dilemma of the contradictories by confining them to matters of the understanding, Hegel and Schelling believed they had gained the open field. They taught that in the highest domain of thought, there where it deals with questions of pure reason, the unity and limits which must be observed in matters of the understanding and which give validity to this third law, do not obtain. This view has been closely criticized, and, I think, with justice.

Pretending to deal with matters of pure reason, it constantly though surreptitiously proceeds on the methods of applied logic; its conclusions are as fallacious logically as they are experimentally. * The laws of thought are formal, and are as binding in transcendental subjects as in those which concern phenomena.

The real bearing of this law can, it appears to me, best be derived from a study of its mathematical expression. This is, according to the notation of Professor Boole, $x^2 = x$. As such, it presents a fundamental equation of thought, and it is because it is of the second degree that we classify in pairs or opposites. This equation can only be satisfied by assigning to x the value of 1 or 0. The " universal type of form" is therefore $x(1-x) = 0$.

This algebraic notation shows that there is, not two, but only one thought in the antithesis; that it is made up of a thought and its expressed limit; and, therefore, that the so-called "law of contradictories" does not concern contradictories at all, in pure logic. This result was seen, though not clearly, by Dr. Thompson, who indicated the proper relation of the members of the formula as a positive and a privative. He, however, retained Hamilton's doctrine that " privative conceptions enter into and assist the higher processes of the reason in all that it can know of the absolute and infinite;" that we must, "from the seen realize an unseen world, not by extending to the latter the properties of the former, but by assigning to it attributes entirely opposite."[1]

The error that vitiates all such reasoning is the assumption that the privative is an independent thought, that a thought and its limitation are two thoughts; whereas they are but the two aspects of the one thought, like two sides to the one disc, and the absurdity of speaking of them as separate thoughts is as great as to speak of a curve seen from its concavity as a different thing from the same curve regarded from its convexity. The privative can help us nowhere and to nothing; the positive only can assist our reasoning.

This elevation of the privative into a contrary, or a contradictory, has been the bane of metaphysical reasoning. From it has arisen the doctrine of the synthesis of an affirmative and a negative into a higher conception, reconciling them both. This is the maxim of the Hegelian logic, which starts from the synthesis of Being and Not-being into the Becoming, a very ancient doctrine, long since offered as an explanation of certain phenomena, which I shall now touch upon.

A thought and its privative alone—that is, a

[1] *An Outline of the Necessary Laws of Thought*, p. 113 (New York, 1860).

quality and its negative—cannot lead to a more comprehensive thought. It is devoid of relation and barren. In pure logic this is always the case, and must be so. In concrete thought it may be otherwise. There are certain propositions in which the negative is a reciprocal quality, quite as positive as that which it is set over against. The members of such a proposition are what are called " true contraries." To whatever they apply as qualities, they leave no middle ground. If a thing is not one of them, it is the other. There is no third possibility. An object is either red or not red ; if not red, it may be one of many colors. But if we say that all laws are either concrete or abstract, then we know that a law not concrete has all the properties of one which is abstract. We must examine, then, this third law of thought in its applied forms in order to understand its correct use.

It will be observed that there is an assumption of space or time in many propositions having the form of the excluded middle. They are only true under given conditions. " All gold is fusible or not," means that some is fusible at the time. If all gold be already fused, it does not hold good. This distinction was noted by Kant in his discrimination between *synthetic* judgments, which assume other conditions ; and *analytic* judgments, which look only at the members of the proposition.

Only the latter satisfy the formal law, for the proposition must not look outside of itself for its completion. Most analytic propositions cannot extend our knowledge beyond their immediate statement. If A is either B or not B, and it is shown not to be B, it is left uncertain what A may be. The class of propositions referred to do more than this, inasmuch as they present alternative conceptions, mutually exhaustive, each the privative of the other. Of these two contraries, the one always evokes the other; neither can be thought except in relation to the other. They do not arise from the dichotomic process of classification, but from the polar relations of things. Their relation is not in the mind but in themselves, a real externality. The distinction between such as spring from the former and the latter is the most important question in philosophy.

To illustrate by examples, we familiarly speak of heat and cold, and to say a body is not hot is as much as to say it is cold. But every physicist knows that cold is merely a diminution of heat, not a distinct form of force. The absolute zero may be reached by the abstraction of all heat, and then the cold cannot increase. So, life and death are not true contraries, for the latter is not anything real but a mere privative, a quantitative diminution of the former, growing less to an absolute zero where it is wholly lost.

Thus it is easy to see that the Unconditioned exists only as a part of the idea of the Conditioned, the Unknowable as the foil of the Knowable; and the erecting of these mere privatives, these negatives, these shadows, into substances and realities, and then setting them up as impassable barriers to human thought, is one of the worst pieces of work that metaphysics has been guilty of.

The like does not hold in true contrasts. Each of them has an existence as a positive, and is never lost in a zero of the other. The one is always thought in relation to the other. Examples of these are subject and object, absolute and relative, mind and matter, person and consciousness, time and space. When any one of these is thought, the other is assumed. It is vain to attempt their separation. Thus those philosophers who assert that all knowledge is relative, are forced to maintain this assertion, to wit, All knowledge is relative, is nevertheless absolute, and thus they falsify their own position. So also, those others who say all mind is a property of matter, assume in this sentence the reality of an idea apart from matter. Some have argued that space and time can be conceived independently of each other; but their experiments to show it do not bear repetition.

All true contraries are universals. A universal concept is one of "maximum extension," as logicians say, that is, it is without limit. The logical limitation of such a universal is not its negation, but its contrary, which is itself also a universal. The synthesis of the two can be in theory only, yet yields a real product. To illustrate this by a geometrical example, a straight line produced indefinitely is, logically considered, a universal. Its antithesis or true contrary is not a crooked line, as might be supposed, but the straight line which runs at right angles to it. Their synthesis is not the line which bisects their angle but that formed by these contraries continually uniting, that is, the arc of a circle, the genesis of which is theoretically the union of two such lines. Again, time can only be measured by space, space by time; they are true universals and contraries; their synthesis is *motion*, a conception which requires them both and is completed by them. Or again, the philosophical extremes of downright materialism and idealism are each wholly true, yet but half the truth. The insoluble enigmas that either meets in standing alone are kindred to those which puzzled the old philosophers in the sophisms relating to motion, as, for instance, that as a body cannot move where it is and still less where it is not, therefore it cannot move at all. Motion must recognise both time and space to be comprehensible. As a true contrary constantly implies the existence of its opposite, we cannot take a step in right reasoning without a full recognition of both.

This relation of contraries to the higher conception which logically must include them is one of the well-worn problems of the higher metaphysics.

The proper explanation would seem to be, as suggested above, that the synthesis of contraries is capable of formal expression only, but not of interpretation. In pursuing the search for their union we pass into a realm of thought not unlike that of the mathematician when he deals with hypothetical quantities, those which can only be expressed in symbols—, $\sqrt{1}$ for example, —but uses them to good purpose in reaching real results. The law does not fail, but its operations can no longer be expressed under material images. They are symbolic and for speculative thought alone, though pregnant with practical applications.

As I have hinted, in all real contraries it is theoretically possible to accept either the one or the other. As in mathematics, all motion can be expressed either under formulæ of initial motion (mechanics), or of continuous motion (kinematics), or as all force can be expressed as either static or as dynamic force; in either case the other form assuming a merely hypothetical or negative position; so the logic of quality is competent to represent all existence as ideal or as material, all truth as absolute or all as relative, or even to express the universe in formulæ of being or of not-being. This perhaps was what Heraclitus meant when he propounded his dark saying: " All things are *and are not.*" He added that " All is not." is truer than " All is." Previous to his day, Buddha Sakyamuni had said: " He who has risen to the perception of the not-Being, to the Unconditioned, the Universal, his path is difficult to understand, like the flight of birds in the air." [1] Perhaps even he learned his lore from some older song of the Veda, one of which ends, " Thus have the sages, meditating in their souls, explained away the fetters of being by the not-being." [2] The not-being, as alone free from space and time, impressed these sages as the more real of the two, the only absolute.

The error of assigning to the one universal a preponderance over the other arose from the easy confusion of pure with applied thought. The synthesis of contraries exists in the formal law alone, and this is difficult to keep before the mind. In concrete displays they are forever incommensurate. One seems to exclude the other. To see them correctly we must there treat them as alternates. We may be competent,

---

[1] *The Dhamapada*, verse 93.
[2] Koppen, *Der Buddhismus*, s. 30.

for instance, to explain all phenomena of mind by organic processes; and equally competent to explain all organism as effects of mind; but we must never suppose an immediate identity of the two; this is only to be found in the formal law common to both; still less should we deny the reality of either. Each exhausts the universe; but at every step each presupposes the other; their synthesis is life, a concept hopelessly puzzling unless regarded in all its possible displays as made up of both.

This indicates also the limits of explanation. By no means every man's reason knows when it has had enough. The less it is developed, the further is it from such knowledge. This is plainly seen in children, who often do not rest satisfied with a really satisfactory explanation. It is of first importance to be able to recognize what is a good reason.

I may first say what it is *not*. It is not a *cause*. This is nothing more than a prior arrangement of the effect; the reason for an occurrence is never assigned by showing its cause. Nor is it a *caprice*, that is, motiveless volition, or will as a motor. In this sense, the "will of God" is no good reason for an occurrence. Nor is it *fate*, or physical necessity. This is denying there is any explanation to give.

The reason can only be satisfied with an aliment consubstantial with itself. Nothing material like cause, nor anything incomprehensible like caprice, meets its demands. Reason is allied to order, system and purpose above all things. That which most completely answers to these will alone satisfy its requirements. They are for an ideal of order. Their complete satisfaction is obtained in universal types and measures, pure abstractions, which are not and cannot be real. The *formal law* is the limit of explanation of phenomena, beyond which a sound intellect will ask nothing. It fulfils all the requirements of reason, and leaves nothing to be desired.

Those philosophers, such as Herbert Spencer, who teach that there is some incogitable " nature " of something which is the immanent " cause " of phenomena, delude themselves with words. The history and the laws of a phenomenon *are* its nature, and there is no chimerical something beyond them. They are exhaustive. They fully answer the question *why*, as well as the question *how*.[1]

---

[1] Spencer in assuming an "unknowable universal causal agent and source of things," as "the nature of the power manifested in phenomena," and in calling this the idea common to both religion and "ideal science," fell far behind Comte, who expressed the immovable position, not only of positive science but of all intelligence, in these words: " Le véritable esprit positif consiste surtout à substituer toujours l'étude des *lois* invariables des phénomènes à celles de leurs *causes* proprement dites, premières ou finales, en un mot la determina-

For it is important to note that the word "law" is not here used in the sense which Blackstone gives to it, a "rule of conduct;" nor yet in that which science assigns to it, a "physical necessity." Law in its highest sense is the type or form, perceived by reason as that toward which phenomena tend, but which they always fail to reach. It was shown by Kant that all physical laws depend for their validity on logical laws. These are not authoritative, like the former, but purposive only. But their purpose is clear, to wit, the attainment of proportion, consistency or truth. As this purpose is reached only in the abstract form, this alone gives us the absolutely true in which reason can rest.

In the concrete, matter shows the law in its efforts toward form, mind in its struggle for the true. The former is guided by physical force, and the extinction of the aberrant. The latter, in its highest exhibition in a conscious intelligence, can alone guide itself by the representation of law, by the sense of Duty. Such an intelligence has both the faculty to see and the power to choose and appropriate to its own be-

---

tion du *comment* à celle du *pourquoi*."—*Systèmede Politique Positive*, i. p. 47. Compare Spencer's Essay entitled, "Reasons for dissenting from Comte." The purposive law is the only final cause which reason allows. Comte's error lay in ignoring this class of laws.

hoof, and thus to build itself up out of those truths which are "from everlasting unto everlasting."

A purely formal truth of this kind as something wholly apart from phenomena, not in any way connected with the knowledge derived through the senses, does not admit of doubt and can never be changed by future conquests of the reasoning powers. We may rest upon it as something more permanent than matter, greater than Nature.

Such was the vision that inspired the noble lines of Wordsworth:—

> "What are things eternal?—Powers depart,
> Possessions vanish, and opinions change,
> And passions hold a fluctuating seat;
> But, by the storms of circumstance unshaken,
> And subject neither to eclipse nor wane,
> Duty exists; immutably survive
> For our support, the measures and the forms
> Which an abstract intelligence supplies;
> Whose kingdom is where time and space are not."

There is no danger that we shall not know what is thus true when we see it. The sane reason cannot reject it. "The true," says Novalis, "is that which we cannot help believing." It is the *perceptio per solam essentiam* of Spinoza. It asks not faith nor yet testimony; it stands in need of neither.

Mathematical truth is of this nature. We

cannot, if we try, believe that twice two is five. Hence the unceasing effort of all science is to give its results mathematical expression. Such truth so informs itself with will that once received, it is never thereafter alienated; obedience to it does not impair freedom. Necessity and servitude do not arise from correct reasoning, but through the limitation of fallacies. They have nothing to do with

> "Those transcendent truths
> Of the pure intellect, that stand as laws
> Even to Thy Being's infinite majesty."

It is not derogatory, but on the contrary essential to the conception of the Supreme Reason, the Divine Logos, to contemplate its will as in accord and one with the forms of abstract truth. "The 'will of God'" says Spinoza, "is the refuge of ignorance; the true Will is the spirit of right reasoning."

This identification of the forms of thought with the Absolute is almost as old as philosophy itself. The objections to it have been that no independent existence attaches to these forms; that they prescribe the conditions of thought but are not thought itself, still less being; that they hold good to thought as known to man's reason, but perchance not to thought in other intelligences; and, therefore, that even if through the dialectical development of thought a consistent idea of the universe were framed, that is, one wherein every fact was referred to its appropriate law, still would remain the inquiry, Is this the last and absolute truth?

The principal points in these objections are that abstract thought does not postulate being; and that possibly all intelligence is not one in kind. To the former objection the most satisfactory reply has been offered by Professor J. F. Ferrier. He has shown that the conception of object, even ideal object, implies the conception of self in the subject; and upon this proposition which has been fully recognized even by those who differ from him widely, he grounds the existence of Supreme Thought as a logical unity. Those who would pursue this branch of the subject further, I would refer to his singularly able work.[1]

The latter consideration will come up in a later chapter. If it be shown that all possible intelligence proceeds on the same laws as that of man, and that the essence of this is activity, permanence, or truth—synonymous terms—then the limitation of time ceases, and existence not in time but without regard to time, is a necessary consequence. Knowledge through intellection can alone reach a truth independent of time; that through sensation is always relative, true

[1] *The Institutes of Metaphysic*, 2d Ed. See also Bain, *The Emotions and the Will*, the closing note.

for the time only. The former cannot be expressed without the implication of the conceptions of the universal and the eternal as " dominant among the subjects of thought with which Logic is concerned;"[1] and hence the relation which the intellect bears to the absolute is a real and positive one.

[1] Boole, *Laws of Thought*, p. 401.

THE EMOTIONAL ELEMENTS OF THE RELIGIOUS SENTIMENT.

SUMMARY.

The Religious Sentiment is made up of emotions and thoughts. The emotions are historically first and most prominent. Of all concerned, Fear is the most obvious. Hope is its correlate. Both suppose Experience, and a desire to repeat or avoid it. Hence a Wish is the source of both emotions, and the proximate element of religion. The significance of desire as the postulate of development. The influence of fear and hope. The conditions which encourage them.

The success of desire fails to gratify the religious sentiment. The alternative left is eternal repose, or else action, unending yet which aims at nothing beyond. The latter is reached through Love. The result of love is *continuance*. Illustrations of this. Sexual love and the venereal sense in religions. The hermaphrodite gods. The virgin mother. Mohammed was the first to proclaim a deity above sex. The conversion of sexual and religious emotion exemplified from insane delusions. The element of fascination. The love of God. Other emotional elements in religions.

The religious wish defined to be one *whose fruition depends upon unknown power*. To be religious, one must desire and be ignorant. The unknown power is of religious interest only in so far as it is believed to be in relation to men's desires. In what sense ignorance is the mother of devotion.

CHAPTER II.

THE EMOTIONAL ELEMENTS OF THE RELIGIOUS SENTIMENT.

THE discussion in the last chapter illustrated how closely pain and pleasure, truth and error, and thought and its laws have been related to the forms of religions, and their dogmatic expressions. The character of the relatively and absolutely true was touched upon, and the latter, it was indicated, if attainable at all by human intelligence, must be found in the formal laws of that intelligence, those which constitute its nature and essence, and in the conclusions which such a premise forces upon the reason. The necessity of this preliminary inquiry arose from the fact that every historical religion claims the monopoly of the absolutely true, and such claims can be tested only when we have decided as to whether there is such truth, and if there is, where it is to be sought. Moreover, as religions arise from some mental demand, the different manifestations of mind,—sensation, emotion and intellect—must be recognized and understood.

Passing now to a particular description of the

Religious Sentiment, it may roughly be defined to be the feeling which prompts to thoughts or acts of worship. It is, as I have said, a complex product, made up of emotions and ideas, developing with the growth of mind, wide-reaching in its maturity, but meagre enough at the start. We need not expect to find in its simplest phases that insight and tender feeling which we attribute to the developed religious character. "The scent of the blossom is not in the bulb." Its early and ruder forms, however, will best teach the mental elements which are at its root.

The problem is, to find out why the primitive man figured to himself any gods at all; what necessity of his nature or his condition led him so universally to assume their existence, and seek their aid or their mercy? The conditions of the solution are, that it hold good everywhere and at all times; that it enable us to trace in every creed and cult the same sentiments which first impelled man to seek a god and adore him. Why is it that now and in remotest history, here and in the uttermost regions, there is and always has been this that we call *religion?* There must be some common reason, some universal peculiarity in man's mental formation which prompts, which forces him, him alone of animals, and him without exception, to this discourse and observance of religion. What this is, it is my present purpose to try to find out.

In speaking of the development of mind through organism, it was seen that the emotions precede the reason in point of time. This is daily confirmed by observation. The child is vastly more emotional than the man, the savage than his civilized neighbor. Castren, the Russian traveller, describes the Tartars and Lapps as a most nervous folk. When one shocks them with a sudden noise, they almost fall into convulsions. Among the North American Indians, falsely called a phlegmatic race, nervous diseases are epidemic to an almost unparalleled extent. Intense thought, on the other hand, as I have before said, tends to lessen and annul the emotions. Intellectual self-consciousness is adverse to them.

But religion, we are everywhere told, is largely a matter of the emotions. The pulpit constantly resounds with appeals to the feelings, and not unfrequently with warnings against the intellect. "I acknowledge myself," says the pious non-juror, William Law, "a declared enemy to the use of reason in religion;" and he often repeats his condemnation of "the labor-learned professors of far-fetched book-riches."[1] As the eye is the organ of sight, says one whose thoughts on such matters equal in depth those of Pascal, so the heart is the organ of religion.[2]

---

[1] *Address to the Clergy*, pp. 42, 43, 67, 106, etc.
[2] F. von Hardenberg [Novalis], *Werke*, s. 361.

In popular physiology, the heart is the seat of the emotions as the brain is that of intellect. It is appropriate, therefore, that we commence our analysis of the religious sentiment with the emotions which form such a prominent part of it.

Now, whether we take the experience of an individual or the history of a tribe, whether we have recourse to the opinions of religious teachers or irreligious philosophers, we find them nigh unanimous that the emotion which is the prime motor of religious thought is *fear*. I need not depend upon the well-known line of Petronius Arbiter,

> Primus in orbe deos fecit timor;

for there is plenty of less heterodox authority. The worthy Bishop Hall says, "Seldom doth God seize upon the heart without a vehement concussion going before. There must be some blustering and flashes of the law. We cannot be too awful in our fear."[1] Bunyan, in his beautiful allegory of the religious life, lets Christian exclaim: "Had even Obstinate himself felt what I have felt of the terrors of the yet unseen, he would not thus lightly have given us the *back*." The very word for God in the Semitic tongues means "fear;"[2] Jacob swore to Laban, "by

---

[1] *Treatises Devotional and Practical*, p. 188. London, 1836.

[2] In Aramaic *dachla* means either a god or fear. The Arabic Allah and the Hebrew Eloah are by some traced to a common

Him whom Isaac feared;" and Moses warned his people that "God is come, that his fear may be before your faces." To *venerate* is from a Sanscrit root (*sêv*), to be afraid of.

But it is needless to amass more evidence on this point. Few will question that fear is the most prominent emotion at the awakening of the religious sentiments. Let us rather proceed to inquire more minutely what fear is.

I remarked in the previous chapter that "the emotions fall naturally into a dual classification, in which the one involves pleasurable or elevating, the other painful or depressing conditions." Fear comes of course under the latter category, as it is essentially a painful and depressing state of mind. But it corresponds with and implies the presence of Hope, for he who has nothing to hope has nothing to fear.[1] "There is no hope without fear, as there is no fear without hope," says Spinoza. "For he who is in fear has some doubt whether what he fears will take place, and consequently hopes that it will not."

We can go a step further, and say that in the mental process the hope must necessarily precede the fear. In the immediate moment of losing a pleasurable sensation we hope and seek

---

root, signifying to tremble, to show fear, though the more usual derivation is from one meaning to be strong.

[1] "Wen die Hoffnung, den hat auch die Furcht verlassen." Arthur Schopenhauer, *Parerga und Paralipomena*. Bd. ii. s. 474.

for its repetition. The mind, untutored by experience, confidently looks for its return. The hope only becomes dashed by fear when experience has been associated with disappointment. Hence we must first look to enjoy a good before we can be troubled by a fear that we shall not enjoy it; we must first lay a plan before we can fear its failure. In modern Christianity hope, hope of immortal happiness, is more conspicuous than fear; but that hope is also based on the picture of a pleasant life made up from experience.

Both hope and fear, therefore, have been correctly called secondary or derived emotions, as they presuppose experience and belief, experience of a pleasure akin to that which we hope, belief that we can attain such a pleasure. " We do not hope first and enjoy afterwards, but we enjoy first and hope afterwards."[1] Having enjoyed, we seek to do so again. A desire, in other words, must precede either Hope or Fear. They are twin sisters, born of a Wish.

Thus my analysis traces the real source of the religious sentiment, so far as the emotions are concerned, to a Wish; and having arrived there, I find myself anticipated by the words of one of the most reflective minds of this century:

---

[1] Alexander Bain, *On the Study of Character*, p. 128. See also his remarks in his work, *The Emotions and the Will*, p. 84, and in his notes to James Mill's *Analysis of the Mind*, vol. i., pp. 124-125.

"All religion rests on a mental want; we hope, we fear, because we wish."[1] And long before this conclusion was reached by philosophers, it had been expressed in unconscious religious thought in myths, in the Valkyria, the Wish-maidens, for instance, who carried the decrees of Odin to earth.

This is no mean origin, for a wish, a desire, conscious or unconscious, in sensation only or in emotion as well, is the fundamental postulate of every sort of development, of improvement, of any possible future, of life of any kind, mental or physical. In its broadest meaning, science and history endorse the exclamation of the unhappy Obermann: "*La perte vraiment irréparable est celle des désirs.*"[2]

The sense of unrest, the ceaseless longing for something else, which is the general source of all desires and wishes, is also the source of all endeavor and of all progress. Physiologically, it is the effort of our organization to adapt itself to the ever varying conditions which surround it; intellectually, it is the struggle to arrive at truth; in both, it is the effort to attain a fuller life.

As stimuli to action, therefore, the commonest and strongest of all emotions are Fear

---

[1] Wilhelm von Humboldt's *Gesammelte Werke*, Bd. vii., s. 62.

[2] De Senancourt, *Obermann*, Lettre xli.

and Hope. They are the emotional correlates of pleasure and pain, which rule the life of sensation. Their closer consideration may well detain us awhile.

In the early stages of religious life, whether in an individual or a nation, the latter is half concealed. Fear is more demonstrative, and as it is essentially destructive, its effects are more sudden and visible. In its acuter forms, as Fright and Terror, it may blanch the hair in a night, blight the mind and destroy the life of the individual. As Panic, it is eminently epidemic, carrying crowds and armies before it; while in the aggravated form of Despair it swallows up all other emotions and prompts to self destruction. Its physiological effect is a direct impairment of vitality.

Hope is less intense and more lasting than fear. It stimulates the system, elates with the confidence of control, strengthens with the courage derived from a conviction of success, and bestows in advance the imagined joy of possession. As Feuchtersleben happily expresses it: "Hope preserves the principle of duration when other parts are threatened with destruction, and is a manifestation of the innermost psychical energy of Life." [1]

Both emotions powerfully prompt to action,

---

[1] *Elements of Medical Psychology*, p. 331.

and to that extent are opposed to thought. Based on belief, they banish uncertainty, and antagonize doubt and with it investigation. The religion in which they enter as the principal factors will be one intolerant of opposition, energetic in deed, and generally hostile to an unbiased pursuit of the truth.

Naturally those temperaments and those physical conditions which chiefly foster these emotions will tend to religious systems in which they are prominent. Let us see what some of these conditions are.

It has always been noticed that impaired vitality predisposes to fear. The sick and feeble are more timorous than the strong and well. Further predisposing causes of the same nature are insufficient nourishment, cold, gloom, malaria, advancing age and mental worry. For this reason nearly invariably after a general financial collapse we witness a religious "revival." Age, full of care and fear, is thus prompted to piety, willing, as La Rochefoucauld remarks, to do good by precept when it can no longer do evil by example. The inhabitants of swampy, fever-ridden districts are usually devout. The female sex, always the weaker and often the worsted one in the struggle for existence, is when free more religious than the male; but with them hope is more commonly the incentive than fear.

Although thus prominent and powerful, desire, so far as its fruition is pleasure, has expressed but the lowest emotions of the religious sentiment. Something more than this has always been asked by sensitively religious minds. Success fails to bring the gratification it promises. The wish granted, the mind turns from it in satiety. Not this, after all, was what we sought.

The acutest thinkers have felt this. Pascal in his *Pensées* has such expressions as these: "The present is never our aim. The future alone is our object." "Forever getting ready to be happy, it is certain we never can be." "'Tis the combat pleases us and not the victory. As soon as that is achieved, we have had enough of the spectacle. So it is in play, so it is in the search for truth. We never pursue objects, but we pursue the pursuit of objects." But no one has stated it more boldly than Lessing when he wrote: "If God held in his right hand all truth, and in his left the one unceasingly active desire for truth, although bound up with the law that I should forever err, I should choose with humility the left and say: 'Give me this, Father. The pure truth is for thee alone.'"[1] The pleasure seems to lie not in the booty but in the battle, not in gaining the stakes but in playing the

---

[1] Lessing's *Gesammelte Werke*. B. ii. s. 443 (Leipzig, 1855).

game, not in the winning but in the wooing, not in the discovery of truth but in the search for it.

What is left for the wise, but to turn, as does the preacher, from this delusion of living, where laughter is mad and pleasure is vain, and praise the dead which are dead more than the living which are yet alive, or to esteem as better than both he that hath never been?

Such is the conclusion of many faiths. Wasted with combat, the mortal longs for the rest prepared for the weary. Buddha taught the extinguishment in Nirvana; the Brahman portrays the highest bliss as *shanti*, complete and eternal repose; and that the same longing was familiar to ancient Judaism, and has always been common to Christianity, numerous evidences testify.[1] Few epitaphs are more common than those which speak of the mortal resting *in pace, in quiete*.

The supposition at the root of these longings is that action must bring fatigue and pain, and though it bring pleasure too, it is bought too dearly. True in fact, I have shown that this conflicts with the theory of perfect life, even organic life. The highest form of life is the most unceasing living; its functions ask for their

---

[1] See Exodus, xxiii. 12; Psalms, lv. 6; Isaiah, xxx. 15; Jeremiah, vi. 16; Hebrews, v. 9. So St. Augustine: "et nos post opera nostra sabbato vitæ eternæ requiescamus in te." *Confessionum Lib.* xiii. cap. 36.

completest well being constant action, not satisfaction. That general feeling of health and strength, that *sens de bien être*, which goes with the most perfect physical life, is experienced only when all the organs are in complete working order and doing full duty. They impart to the whole frame a desire of motion. Hence the activity of the young and healthy as contrasted with the inertness of the exhausted and aged.

How is it possible to reconcile this ideal of life, still more the hope of everlasting life, with the acknowledged vanity of desire? It is accomplished through the medium of an emotion which more than any I have touched upon reveals the character of the religious sentiment —Love. This mighty but protean feeling I shall attempt to define on broader principles than has hitherto been done. The vague and partial meanings assigned it have led to sad confusion in the studies of religions. In the language of feeling, love is a passion; but it does not spring from feeling alone. It is far more fervid when it rises through intellect than through sense. "Men have died from time to time, and worms have eaten them, but not for love," says the fair Rosalind; and though her saying is not very true as to the love of sense, it is far less true as to the love of intellect. The martyrs to science and religion, to principles and faith, multiply a hundred-fold those to the garden god. The spell of the idea is what

"Turns ruin into laughter and death into dreaming."

Such love destroys the baser passion of sense, or transfigures it so that we know it no longer. The idea-driven is callous to the blandishments of beauty, for his is a love stronger than the love to woman. The vestal, the virgin, the eunuch for the kingdom of heaven's sake are the exemplars of the love to God.

What common trait so marks these warring products of mind, that we call them by one name? In what is all love the same? The question is pertinent, for the love of woman, the love of neighbor, the love of country, the love of God, have made the positive side of most religions, the burden of their teachings. The priests of Cotytto and Venus, Astarte and Melitta, spoke but a more sensuous version of the sermon of the aged apostle to the Ephesians, —shortest and best of all sermons—"Little children, love one another."[1]

The earliest and most constant sign of reason is "working for a remote object."[2] Nearly everything we do is as a step to something beyond. Forethought, conscious provision, is the

---

[1] "Filioli, diligite alterutrum." This is the "testamentum Johannis," as recorded from tradition by St. Jerome in his notes to the Epistle to the Galatians.

[2] Alexander Bain, *The Senses and the Intellect*, Chap. I.

measure of intelligence. But there must be something which is the object, the aim, the end-in-view of rational action, which is sought for itself alone, not as instrumental to something else. Such an object, when recognized, inspires the sentiment of love. It springs from the satisfaction of reason.

This conclusion as to the nature of love has long been recognized by thinkers. Richard Baxter defined it as " the volition of the end," " the motion of the soul that tendeth to the end," and more minutely, " the will's volition of good apprehended by the understanding." [1] In similar language Bishop Butler explains it as " the resting in an object as an end." [2] Perhaps I can better these explanations by the phrase, *Love is the mental impression of rational action whose end is in itself.*

Now this satisfaction is found only in one class of efforts, namely, those whose result is continuity, persistence, in fine, *preservation*. This may be toward the individual, self-love, whose object is the continuance of personal existence; toward the other sex, where the hidden aim is the perpetuation of the race; toward

---

[1] *A Christian Directory.* Part I. Chap. III.

[2] " The very nature of affection, the idea itself, necessarily implies resting in its object as an end." *Fifteen Sermons by Joseph Butler, late Lord Bishop of Durham*, Preface, and p. 147 (London, 1841).

one's fellows, where the giving of pleasure and the prevention of pain mean the maintenance of life ; toward one's country, as patriotism; and finally toward the eternally true, which as alone the absolutely permanent and preservative, inspires a love adequate and exhaustive of its conception, casting out both hope and fear, the pangs of desire as well as the satiety of fruition.

In one or other of these forms love has at all times been the burden of religion : the glad tidings it has always borne have been "love on earth." The Phœnix in Egyptian myth appeared yearly as newly risen, but was ever the same bird, and bore the egg from which its *parent* was to have birth. So religions have assumed the guise in turn of self-love, sex-love, love of country and love of humanity, cherishing in each the germ of that highest love which alone is the parent of its last and only perfect embodiment.

Favorite of these forms was sex-love. "We find," observes a recent writer, "that all religions have engaged and concerned themselves with the sexual passion. From the times of phallic worship through Romish celibacy down to Mormonism, theology has linked itself with man's reproductive instincts."[1] The remark is just, and is most conspicuously correct in

---

[1] Dr. J. Milner Fothergill, *Journal of Mental Science*, Oct. 1874, p. 198.

strongly emotional temperaments. "The devotional feelings," writes the Rev. Frederick Robertson in one of his essays, "are often singularly allied to the animal nature; they conduct the unconscious victim of feelings that appear divine into a state of life at which the world stands aghast." Fanaticism is always united with either excessive lewdness or desperate asceticism. The physiological performance of the generative function is sure to be attacked by religious bigotry.

So prominent is this feature that attempts have been made to explain nearly all symbolism and mythology as types of the generative procedure and the reproductive faculty of organism. Not only the pyramids and sacred mountains, the obelisks of the Nile and the myths of light have received this interpretation, but even such general symbols as the spires of churches, the cross of Christendom and the crescent of Islam.[1]

Without falling into the error of supposing that any one meaning or origin can be assigned such frequent symbols, we may acknowledge that love, in its philosophical sense, is closely akin to the mystery of every religion. That, on occasions, love of sex gained the mastery over all other forms, is not to be doubted; but that at all times

---

[1] The most recent work on the topic is that of Messrs. Westropp and Wake, *The Influence of the Phallic Idea on the Religions of Antiquity*, London, 1874.

THE GROWTH OF SEX-LOVE. 63

this was so, is a narrow, erroneous view, not consistent with a knowledge of the history of psychical development.

Sex-love, as a sentiment, is a cultivated growth. All it is at first is a rude satisfaction of the erethism. The wild tribes of California had their pairing seasons when the sexes were in heat, "as regularly as the deer, the elk and the antelope."[1] In most tongues of the savages of North America there are no tender words, as "dear," "darling," and the like.[2] No desire of offspring led to their unions. The women had few children, and their fathers paid them little attention. The family instinct appears in conditions of higher culture, in Judea, Greece, Rome and ancient Germany. Procreation instead of lust was there the aim of marriage. To-day, mere sentiment is so much in the ascendant that both these elements are often absent. There is warm affection without even instinctive knowledge of the design of the bond assumed.[3]

Those who would confine the promptings of the passion of reproduction as it appears in man to its objects as shown in lower animals, know

---

[1] Schoolcraft's *History and Statistics of the Indian Tribes*, Vol. iv. p. 224.

[2] Richardson, *Arctic Expedition*, p. 412.

[3] Most physicians have occasion to notice the almost entire loss in modern life of the instinctive knowledge of the sex relation. Sir James Paget has lately treated of the subject in one of his *Clinical Lectures* (London, 1875).

little how this wondrous emotion has acted as man's mentor as well as paraclete in his long and toilsome conflict with the physical forces.

The venereal sense is unlike the other special senses in that it is general, as well as referable to special organs and nerves. In its psychological action it "especially contributes to the development of sympathies which connect man not only with his coevals, but with his fellows of all preceding and succeeding generations as well. Upon it is erected this vast superstructure of intellect, of social and moral sentiment, of voluntary effort and endeavor."[1] Of all the properties of organized matter, that of transmitting form and life is the most wonderful; and if we examine critically the physical basis of the labors and hopes of mankind, if we ask what prompts its noblest and holiest longings, we shall find them, in the vast majority of instances, directly traceable to this power. No wonder then that religion, which we have seen springs from man's wants and wishes, very often bears the distinct trace of their origin in his reproductive functions. The lions of the family are justly deemed sacred, and are naturally associated with whatever the mind considers holy.

The duty of a citizen to become a father was

[1] Dr. J. P. Catlow, *Principles of Aesthetic Medicine*, p. 112. This thoughtful though obscure writer has received little recognition even in the circle of professional readers.

a prominent feature in many ancient religions. How much honor the sire of many sons had in Rome and Palestine is familiar to all readers. No warrior, according to German faith, could gain entrance to Valhalla unless he had begotten a son. Thus the preservation of the species was placed under the immediate guardianship of religion.

Such considerations explain the close connection of sexual thoughts with the most sacred mysteries of faith. In polytheisms, the divinities are universally represented as male or female, virile and fecund. The processes of nature were often held to be maintained through such celestial nuptials.

Yet stranger myths followed those of the loves of the gods. Religion, as the sentiment of continuance, finding its highest expression in the phenomenon of generation, had to reconcile this with the growing concept of a divine unity. Each separate god was magnified in praises as self-sufficient. Earth, or nature, or the season is one, yet brings forth all. How embody this in concrete form?

The startling refuge was had in the image of a deity at once of both sexes. Such avowedly were Mithras, Janus, Melitta, Cybele, Aphrodite, Agdistis; indeed nearly all the Syrian, Egyptian, and Italic gods, as well as Brahma, and, in the esoteric doctrine of the Cabala, even Jehovah, whose female aspect is represented by the

"Shekinah." To this abnormal condition the learned have applied the adjectives epicene, androgynous, hermaphrodite, arrenothele. In art it is represented by a blending of the traits of both sexes. In the cult it was dramatically set forth by the votaries assuming the attire of the other sex, and dallying with both.[1] The phallic symbol superseded all others; and in Cyprus, Babylonia and Phrygia, once in her life, at least, must every woman submit to the embrace of a stranger.

Such rites were not mere sensualities. The priests of these divinities often voluntarily suffered emasculation. None but a eunuch could become high priest of Cybele. Among the sixteen million worshippers of Siva, whose symbol is the Lingam, impurity is far less prevalent than among the sister sects of Hindoo religions.[2] To the Lingayets, the member typifies abstractly the idea of life. Therefore they carve it on sepulchres, or, like the ancient nations of Asia Minor, they lay clay images of it on graves to intimate the hope of existence beyond the tomb.

This notion of a hermaphrodite deity is not "monstrous," as it has been called. There lies

---

[1] This is probably what was condemned in Deuteronomy xxii. 5, and Romans, i. 26.

[2] "The worship of Siva is too severe, too stern for the softer emotions of love, and all his temples are quite free from any allusions to it."—Ferguson, *Tree and Serpent Worship*, p. 71.

a deep meaning in it. The gods are spirits, beings of another order, which the cultivated esthetic sense protests against classing as of one or the other gender. Never can the ideal of beauty, either physical or moral, be reached until the characteristics of sex are lost in the concept of the purely human. In the noblest men of history there has often been noted something feminine, a gentleness which is not akin to weakness; and the women whose names are ornaments to nations have displayed a calm greatness, not unwomanly but something more than belongs to woman. Art acknowledges this. In the Vatican Apollo we see masculine strength united with maidenly softness; and in the traditional face and figure of Christ a still more striking example how the devout mind conjoins the traits of both sexes to express the highest possibility of the species. " Soaring above the struggle in which the real is involved with its limitations, and free from the characteristics of gender, the ideal of beauty as well as the ideal of humanity, alike maintain a perfect sexual equilibrium." [1]

Another and more familiar expression of the religious emotion, akin to the belief in double-

---

[1] W. von Humboldt, in his admirable essay *Ueber die Männliche und Weibliche Form* (*Werke, Bd. I.*). Elsewhere he adds: " In der Natur des Gœttlichen strebt alles der Reinheit und Vollkommenheit des Gattungsbegriff entgegen."

sexed deities,—nay, in its physiological aspect identical with it, as assuming sexual self-sufficiency, is the myth of the Virgin-Mother.

When Columbus first planted the cross on the shores of San Domingo, the lay brother Roman Pane, whom he sent forth to convert the natives of that island, found among them a story of a virgin Mamóna, whose son Yocaúna, a hero and a god, was chief among divinities, and had in the old times taught this simple people the arts of peace and guided them through the islands.[1] When the missionaries penetrated to the Iroquois, the Aztecs, the Mayas, and many other tribes, this same story was told them with such startling likeness to one they came to tell, that they felt certain either St. Thomas or Satan had got the start of them in America.

But had these pious men known as well as we do the gentile religions of the Old World, they would have seasoned their admiration. Long before Christianity was thought of, the myth of the Virgin-Mother of God was in the faith of millions, as we have had abundantly shown us of late years by certain expounders of Christian dogmas.

How is this strange, impossible belief to be

---

[1] I have collected the Haitian myths, chiefly from the manuscript *Historia Apologetica de las Indias Occidentales* of Las Casas, in an essay published in 1871, *The Arawack Language of Guiana in its Linguistic and Ethnological Relations*.

explained? Of what secret, unconscious, psychological working was it the expression? Look at its result. It is that wherever this doctrine is developed the *status matrimonialis* is held to be less pure, less truly religious, than the *status virginitatis*. Such is the teaching to-day in Lhassa, in Rome; so it was in Yucatan, where, too, there were nunneries filled with spouses of God. I connect it with the general doctrine that chastity in either sex is more agreeable to God than marriage, and this belief, I think, very commonly arises at a certain stage of development of the religious sentiment, when it unconsciously recognises the indisputable fact that sex-love, whether in its form of love of woman, family, or nation, is not what that sentiment craves. This is first shown by rejecting the idea of sex-love in the birth of the god; then his priests and priestesses refuse its allurements, and deny all its claims, those of kindred, of country, of race, until the act of generation itself is held unholy and the thought of sex a sin. By such forcible though rude displays do they set forth their unconscious acknowledgment of that eternal truth: "He that loveth son or daughter more than Me, is not worthy of Me."

The significance of these words is not that there is an antagonism in the forms of love. It is not that man should hate himself, as Pascal, following the teachings of the Church, so ably argued; nor that the one sex should be set over against the other in sterile abhorrence; nor yet that love of country and of kindred is incompatible with that toward the Supreme of thought; but it is that each of these lower, shallower, evanescent forms of emotion is and must be lost in, subordinated to, that highest form to which these words have reference. Reconciliation, not abnegation, is what they mean.

Even those religions which teach in its strictness the oneness of God have rarely separated from his personality the attribute of sex. He is the father, *pater et genitor*, of all beings. The monotheism which we find in Greece and India generally took this form. The ancient Hebrews emphasized the former, not the latter sense of the word, and thus depriving it of its more distinctive characteristics of sex, prepared the way for the teachings of Christianity, in which the Supreme Being always appears with the attributes of the male, but disconnected from the idea of generation.

Singularly enough, the efforts to which this latent incongruity prompts, even in persons speaking English, in which tongue the articles and adjectives have no genders, point back to the errors of an earlier age. A recent prayer by an eminent spiritualist commences :—" Oh Eternal Spirit, our Father and our Mother!" The expression illustrates how naturally arises the belief in a hermaphrodite god, when once sex is associated with deity.

Of all founders of religions, Mohammed first proclaimed a divinity without relation to sex. One of his earliest suras reads :

> "He is God alone,
> God the eternal.
> He begetteth not, and is not begotten ;
> And there is none like unto him."

And elsewhere :—

> "He hath no spouse, neither hath he any offspring."[1]

While he expressly acknowledged the divine conception of Jesus, he denied the coarse and literal version of that doctrine in vogue among the ignorant Christians around him. Enlightened christendom, to-day, does not, I believe, differ from him on this point.

Such sexual religions do not arise, as the theory has hitherto been, from study and observation of the generative agencies in nature, but from the identity of object between love in sense and love in intellect, profane and sacred passion. The essence of each is *continuance*, preservation ; the origin of each is subjective, personal; but the former has its root in sensation, the latter in reason.

The sex-difference in organisms, the "abhorrence of self-fertilization" which Mr. Darwin speaks of as so conspicuous and inexplicable a

---

[1] *The Karan*, Suras, cxii., lxii., and especially xix.

phenomenon, is but one example of the sway of a law which as action and reaction, thesis and antithesis, is common to both elementary motion and thought. The fertile and profound fancy of Greece delighted to prefigure this truth in significant symbols and myths. Love, Eros, is shown carrying the globe, or wielding the club of Hercules; he is the unknown spouse of Psyche, the soul; and from the primitive chaos he brings forth the ordered world, the Kosmos.

The intimate and strange relation between sensuality and religion, so often commented upon and denied, again proven, and always misinterpreted, thus receives a satisfactory explanation. Some singular manifestations of it, of significance in religious history, are presented by the records of insane delusions. They confirm what I have above urged, that the association is not one derived from observation through intellectual processes, but is a consequence of physiological connections, of identity of aim in the distinct realms of thought and emotion.

That eminent writer on mental diseases, Schroeder van der Kolk, when speaking of the forms of melancholy which arise from physical conditions, remarks : " The patient who is melancholy from disorders of the generative organs considers himself sinful. His depressed tone of mind passes over into religious melancholy; 'he is forsaken by God; he is lost.' All his afflictions have a religious color." In a similar strain, Feuchtersleben says: "In the female sex especially, the erotic delusion, unknown to the patient herself, often assumes the color of the religious." [1] " The unaccomplished sexual designs of nature," observes a later author speaking of the effects of the single life, "lead to brooding over supposed miseries which suggest devotion and religious exercise as the nepenthe to soothe the morbid longings." [2]

Stimulate the religious sentiment and you arouse the passion of love, which will be directed as the temperament and individual culture prompt. Develope very prominently any one form of love, and by a native affinity it will seize upon and consecrate to its own use whatever religious aspirations the individual has. This is the general law of their relation.

All the lower forms of love point to one to which they are the gradual ascent, both of the individual and on a grander scale of the race, to wit, the love of God. This is the passion for the highest attainable truth, a passion which, as duty, prompts to the strongest action and to the utter sacrifice of all other longings. No speculative acquaintance with propositions satisfies it, no

[1] *Elements of Medical Psychology*, p. 281.

[2] J. Thompson Dickson, *The Science and Practice of Medicine in relation to Mind*, p. 383 (New York, 1874).

egotistic construction of systems, but the truth expressed in life, the truth as that which alone either has or can give being and diuturnity, this is its food, for which it thirsts with holy ardor. Here is the genuine esoteric gnosis, the sacred secret, which the rude and selfish wishes of the savage, the sensual rites of Babylon, "mother of harlots," and the sublimely unselfish dreams of a "religion of humanity," have alike had in their hearts, but had no capacity to interpret, no words to articulate.

Related to this emotional phase of the religious sentiment is the theurgic power of certain natural objects over some persons. The biblical scholar Kitto confesses that the moon exerted a strange influence on his mind, stirring his devotional nature, and he owns that it would not have been hard for him to join the worshippers of the goddess of the night. Wilhelm von Humboldt in one of his odes refers to similar feelings excited in him by the gloom and murmur of groves. The sacred poets and the religious arts generally acknowledge this *fascination*, as it has been called, which certain phenomena have for religious temperaments.

The explanation which suggests itself is that of individual and ancestral association. In the case of Kitto it was probably the latter. His sensitively religious nature experienced in gazing at the moon an impression inherited from some remote ancestor who had actually made it the object of ardent worship. The study of the laws of inherited memory, so successfully pursued of late by Professor Laycock, take away anything eccentric about this explanation, though I scarcely expect it will be received by one unacquainted with those laws.

The emotional aspect of religion is not exhausted by the varieties of fear and hope and love. Wonder, awe, admiration, the æsthetic emotions, in fact all the active principles of man's mental economy are at times excited and directed by the thought of supernatural power. Some have attempted to trace the religious sentiment exclusively to one or the other of these. But they are all incidental and subsidiary emotions.

Certain mental diseases, by abnormally stimulating the emotions, predispose strongly to religious fervor. Epilepsy is one of these, and in Swedenborg and Mohammed, both epileptics, we see distinguished examples of religious mystics, who, no doubt honestly, accepted the visions which accompanied their disease as revelations from another world. Very many epileptics are subject to such delusions, and their insanity is usually of a religious character.

On the other hand, devotional excitement is apt to bring about mental alienation. Every violent revival has left after it a small crop of religious melancholics and lunatics. Competent authorities state that in modern communities religious insanity is most frequent in those sects who are given to emotional forms of religion, the Methodists and Baptists for example; whereas it is least known among Roman Catholics, where doubt and anxiety are at once allayed by an infallible referee, and among the Quakers, where enthusiasm is discouraged and with whom the restraint of emotion is a part of discipline.[1] Authoritative assurance in many disturbed conditions of mind is sufficient to relieve the mental tension and restore health.

If, by what has been said, it is clear that the religious sentiment has its origin in a wish, it is equally clear that not every wish is concerned in it. The objects which a man can attain by his own unaided efforts, are not those which he makes the subjects of his prayers; nor are the periodic and regular occurrences in nature, how impressive they may be, much thought of in devotional moods. The moment that an event is recognized to be under fixed law, it is seen to be inappropriate to seek by supplication to alter it. No devotee, acquainted with the theory of the tides, would, like Canute the King, think of staying their waves with words. Eclipses and

[1] Dr. Joseph Williams, *Insanity, its Causes, Prevention and Cure*, pp. 68, 69; Dr. A. L. Wigan, *The Duality of the Mind*, p. 437.

comets, once matters of superstitious terror, have been entirely shorn of this attribute by astronomical discovery. Even real and tragic misfortunes, if believed to be such as flow from fixed law, and especially if they can be predicted sometime before they arrive, do not excite religious feeling. As Bishop Hall quaintly observes, referring to a curious medieval superstition : " Crosses, after the nature of the cockatrice, die if they be foreseen."

Only when the event suggests the direct action of *mind*, of some free intelligence, is it possible for the religious sentiment to throw around it the aureole of sanctity. Obviously when natural law was little known, this included vastly more occurrences than civilized men now think of holding to be of religious import. Hence the objective and material form of religion is always fostered by ignorance, and this is the form which prevails exclusively in uncultivated societies.

The manifestations of motion which the child first notices, or which the savage chiefly observes, relate to himself. They are associated with the individuals around him who minister to his wants ; the gratification of these depend on the volitions of others. As he grows in strength he learns to supply his own wants, and to make good his own volitions as against those of his fellows. But he soon learns that many events occur to thwart him, out of connection with any known individual, and these of a dreadful nature, hurricanes and floods, hunger, sickness and death. These pursue him everywhere, foiling his plans, and frustrating his hopes. It is not the show of power, the manifestations of might, that he cares for in these events, but that they touch *him*, that they spoil *his* projects, and render vain *his* desires; *this* forces him to cast about for some means to protect himself against them.

In accordance with the teaching of his experience, and true moreover to the laws of mind, he refers them, collectively, to a mental source, to a vague individuality. This loose, undefined conception of an unknown volition or power forms the earliest notion of Deity. It is hardly associated with personality, yet it is broadly separated from the human and the known. In the languages of savage tribes, as I have elsewhere remarked, "a word is usually found comprehending all manifestations of the unseen world, yet conveying no sense of personal unity."[1]

By some means to guard against this undefined marplot to the accomplishment of his wishes, is the object of his religion. Its primitive forms are therefore defensive and conciliatory. The hopes of the savage extend little beyond the reach of his own arm, and the tenor of his

[1] *The Myths of the New World, a Treatise on the Symbolism and Mythology of the Red Race of America*, p. 145.

prayers is that the gods be neuter. If they do not interfere he can take care of himself. His religion is a sort of assurance of life.

Not only the religion of the savage, but every religion is this and not much but this. With nobler associations and purer conceptions of life, the religious sentiment ever contains these same elements and depends upon them for its vigor and growth. It everywhere springs from *a desire whose fruition depends upon unknown power*. To give the religious wish a definition in the technic of psychology, I define it as: *Expectant Attention, directed toward an event not under known control, with a concomitant idea of Cause or Power*.

Three elements are embraced in this definition, a wish, an idea of power, ignorance of the nature of that power. The first term prompts the hope, the third suggests the fear, and the second creates the personality, which we see set forth in every religious system. Without these three, religion as dogma becomes impossible.

If a man wishes for nothing, neither the continuance of present comforts nor future blessings, why need he care for the gods? Who can hurt him, so long as he stays in his frame of mind? He may well shake off all religions and every fear, for he is stronger than God, and the universe holds nothing worth his effort to get. This was the doctrine taught by Buddha Sakyanuni, a philosopher opposed to every form of religion, but who is the reputed founder of the most numerous sect now on the globe. He sought to free the minds of his day from the burden of the Brahmanic ritual, by cultivating a frame of mind beyond desire or admiration, and hence beyond the need of a creed.

The second element, the idea of power, is an intellectual abstraction. Its character is fluctuating. At first it is most vague, corresponding to what in its most general sense we term "the supernatural." Later, it is regarded under its various exhibitions as separable phenomena, as in polytheisms, in which must be included trinitarian systems and the dualistic doctrine of the Parsees. But among the Egyptians, Greeks and Aztecs, as well as in the words of Zarathustra and in the theology of Christianity, we frequently meet with the distinct recognition of the fundamental unity of all power. At core, all religions have seeds of monotheism. When we generalize the current concepts of motion or force beyond individual displays and relative measures of quantity, we recognize their qualitative identity, and appreciate the logical unity under which we must give them abstract expression. This is the process, often unconscious, which has carried most original thinkers to monotheistic doctrines, no matter whence they started.

The idea of power controlling the unknown

would of itself have been of no interest to man had he not assumed certain relations to exist between him and it on the one hand, and it and things on the other. A dispassionate inquiry disproves entirely the view maintained by various modern writers, prominently by Bain, Spencer and Darwin, that the contemplation of power or majesty in external nature prompts of itself the religious sentiment, or could have been its historical origin. Such a view overlooks the most essential because the personal factor of religion—the wish. Far more correct are the words of David Hume, in the last century, by which he closes his admirable *Natural History of Religions:* "We may conclude, therefore, that in all nations the first ideas of religion arose not from a contemplation of the works of nature, but from a concern with regard to the events of life, and from the incessant hopes and fears which actuate the human mind." A century before him Hobbes had written in his terse way: "The natural seed of religion lies in these four things: the fear of spirits, ignorance of secondary causes, the conciliation of those we fear, and the assumption of accidents for omens."[1] The sentiment of religion is in its origin and nature purely personal and subjective. The aspect of power would never have led man to worship, unless he had assumed certain relations between

[1] *Leviathan, De Homine,* cap. xii.

the unseen author or authors of that power and himself. What these assumptions were, I shall discuss in the next chapter.

Finally, as has so often been remarked in a flippant and contemptuous way,[1] which the fact when rightly understood nowise justifies, religion cannot exist without the aid of ignorance. It is really and truly the mother of devotion. The sentiment of religious fear does not apply to a *known* power—to the movement of an opposing army, or the action of gravity in an avalanche for example. The prayer which under such circumstances is offered, is directed to an unknown intelligence, supposed to control the visible forces. As science—which is the knowledge of physical laws—extends, the object of prayer becomes more and more intangible and remote. What we formerly feared, we learn to govern. No one would pray God to avert the thunderbolt, if lightning rods invariably protected houses. The Swiss clergy opposed the system of insuring growing crops because it made their parishioners indifferent to prayers for the harvest. With increasing knowledge

[1] For instance, of later writers from whom we might expect better things, Arthur Schopenhauer. He says in his *Parerga* (Bd. ii. s. 290): "Ein gewisser Grad allgemeiner Unwissenheit ist die Bedingung aller Religionen;" a correct remark, and equally correct of the pursuit of science and philosophy. But the ignorance which is the condition of such pursuit is not a part of science or philosophy, and no more is it of religion.

and the security which it brings, religious terror lessens, and the wants which excite the sentiment of devotion diminish in number and change in character.

This is apt to cast general discredit on religion. When we make the discovery that so many events which excited religious apprehension in the minds of our forefathers are governed by inflexible laws which we know all about, we not only smile in pity at their superstitions, but make the mental inference that the diminished emotion of this kind we yet experience is equally groundless. If at the bottom of all displays of power lies a physical necessity, our qualms are folly. Therefore, to the pious soul which still finds the bulk of its religious aspirations and experiences in the regions of the emotions and sensations, the progress of science seems and really does threaten its cherished convictions. The audacious mind of man robs the gods of power when he can shield himself from their anger. The much-talked-of conflict between religion and science is no fiction; it exists, and is bound to go on, and religion will ever get the worst of it until it learns that the wishes to which it is its proper place to minister are not those for pleasure and prosperity, not for abundant harvests and seasonable showers, not success in battle and public health, not preservation from danger and safety on journeys, not much of anything that is spoken of in litanies and books of devotion.

Let a person who still clings to this form of religion imagine that science had reached perfection in the arts of life; that by skilled adaptations of machinery, accidents by sea and land were quite avoided; that observation and experience had taught to foresee with certainty and to protect effectively against all meteoric disturbances; that a perfected government insured safety of person and property; that a consummate agriculture rendered want and poverty unknown; that a developed hygiene completely guarded against disease; and that a painless extinction of life in advanced age could surely be calculated upon; let him imagine this, and then ask himself what purpose religion would subserve in such a state of things? For whatever would occupy it then—if it could exist at all—should *alone* occupy it now.

THE RATIONAL POSTULATES OF THE RELIGIOUS SENTIMENT.

SUMMARY.

Religion often considered merely an affair of the feelings. On the contrary, it must assume at least three premises in reason, its "rational postulates."

1. There is Order in things.

The religious wish involves the idea of cause. This idea not exhausted by uniformity of sequence, but by quantitative relation, that is, Order as opposed to Chance. Both science and religion assume order in things; but the latter includes the Will of God in this order, while the former rejects it.

II. This order is one of Intelligence.

The order is assumed to be a comprehensible one, whether it be of law wholly or of volition also.

III. All Intelligence is one in kind.

This postulate indispensable to religion, although it has been attacked by religious as well as irreligious philosophers. Its decision must rest on the absoluteness of the formal laws of thought. The theory that these are products of natural selection is disproved by showing, (1) that they hold true throughout the material universe, and (2) that they do not depend on it for their verity. Reason sees beyond phenomena, but descries nothing alien to itself.

The formal laws of reason are purposive. They therefore afford a presumption of a moral government of the Universe, and point to an Intelligence fulfilling an end through the order in physical laws. Such an assumption, common to all historic religions, is thus justified by induction.

CHAPTER III.

THE RATIONAL POSTULATES OF THE RELIGIOUS SENTIMENT.

In philosophical discussions of religion as well as in popular exhortations upon it, too exclusive stress has been laid upon its emotional elements. "It is," says Professor Bain, "an affair of the feelings."[1] "The essence of religion," observes John Stuart Mill, "is the strong and earnest direction of the emotions and desires towards an ideal object." "It must be allowed," says Dr. Mansel,[2] "that it is not through reasoning that men obtain their first intimation of their relation to a deity." In writers and preachers of the semi-mystical school, which embraces most of the ardent revivalists of the day, we constantly hear the "feeling of dependence" quoted as the radical element of religious thought.[3] In

---

[1] *The Emotions and Will*, p. 594. So Professor Tyndall speaks of confining the religious sentiment to "the region of emotion, which is its proper sphere."

[2] H. L. Mansel, *The Limits of Religious Thought*, p. 115. (Boston, 1859.)

[3] "The *one relation* which is the ground of all true religion is a total dependence upon God." William Law, *Address to the Clergy*, p. 12. "The essential germ of the religious life is con-

America Theodore Parker, and in Germany Schleiermacher, were brilliant exponents of this doctrine. To the latter the philosopher Hegel replied that if religion is a matter of feeling, an affectionate dog is the best Christian.

This answer was not flippant, but founded on the true and only worthy conception of the religious sentiment. We have passed in review the emotions which form a part of it, and recognize their power. But neither these nor any other mere emotions, desires or feelings can explain even the lowest religion. It depends for its existence on the essential nature of reason. We cannot at all allow, as Dr. Mansel asks of us, that man's first intimations of Deity came in any other way than as one of the ripest fruits of reason. Were such the case, we should certainly find traces of them among brutes and idiots, which we do not. The slight signs of religious actions thought to have been noticed by some in the lower animals, by Sir John Lubbock in ants, and by Charles Darwin in dogs, if authenticated, would vindicate for these species a much closer mental kinship to man than we have yet supposed.

If we dispassionately analyze any religion

centrated in the absolute feeling of dependence on infinite power." J. D. Morell, *The Philosophy of Religion*, p. 94. (New York, 1849.) This accomplished author, well known for his *History of Philosophy*, is the most able English exponent of the religious views of Schleiermacher and Jacobi.

whatever, paying less attention to what its professed teachers say it is, than to what the mass of the votaries believe it to be, we shall see that every form of adoration unconsciously assumes certain premises in reason, which give impulse and character to its emotional and active manifestations. They are its data or axioms, or, as I shall call them, its " rational postulates." They can, I believe, be reduced to three, but not to a lesser number.

Before the religious feeling acquires the distinctness of a notion and urges to conscious action, it must assume at least these three postulates, and without them it cannot rise into cognition. These, their necessary character and their relations, I shall set forth in this chapter.

They are as follows:—

    I. There is Order in things.
    II. This order is one of Intelligence.
    III. All Intelligence is one in kind.

I. The conscious or unconscious purpose of the religious sentiment, as I have shown in the last chapter, is the *fruition of a wish*, the success of which depends upon unknown power. The votary asks help where he cannot help himself. He expects it through an exertion of power, through an efficient cause. Obviously therefore, he is acting on the logical idea of Causality. This underlies and is essential to the simplest prayer. He extends it, moreover, out of the limits of experience into the regions of hypothesis. He has carried the analogy of observation into the realm of abstract conceptions. No matter if he does believe that the will of God is the efficient cause. Perhaps he is right; at any rate he cannot be denied the privilege of regarding volition as a co-operating cause. Limited at first to the transactions which most concerned men, the conception of order as a divine act extended itself to the known universe. Herodotus derives the Greek word for God (θεος) from a root which gives the meaning "to set in order," and the Scandinavians gave the same sense to their word, *Regin*.[1] Thus the abstract idea of cause or power is a postulate of all religious thought. Let us examine its meaning.

Every reader, the least versed in the history of speculative thought for the last hundred years, knows how long and violent the discussions have been of the relations of "cause and effect." Startled by the criticisms of Hume, Kant sought to elude them by distinguishing between two spheres of thought, the understanding and the reason. Sir William Hamilton at

[1] "Weil sie die Welt *eingerichtet* haben." Creuzer, *Symbolik und Mythologie der alten Völker*, Bd. I. s. 169. It is not of any importance that Herodotus' etymology is incorrect : what I wish to show is that he and his contemporaries entertained the conception of the gods as the authors of order.

first included the " principle of sufficient reason' in the laws of thought, but subsequently rejected it as pertaining to judgments, and therefore material, not formal. Schopenhauer claimed to have traced it to a fourfold root, and Mill with most of the current English schools, Bain, Austin, Spencer, &c., maintained that it meant nothing but "uniformity of sequence."

It would be vain to touch upon a discussion so extended as this. In the first chapter I have remarked that the idea of cause does not enter into the conceptions of pure logic or thought. It is, as Hamilton saw, material. I shall only pause to show what is meant by the term "cause" in the physical sciences. When one event follows another, time after time, we have " uniformity of sequence." Suppose the constitution of the race were so happy that we slept at night only, and always awoke a few moments before sunrise. Such a sequence quite without exception, should, if uniform experience is the source of the idea of cause, justly lead to the opinion that the sun rises because man awakes. As we know this conclusion would be erroneous, some other element beside sequence must complete a real cause. If now, it were shown that the relation of cause to effect which we actually entertain and cannot help entertaining is in some instances flatly contrary to all experience, then we must acknowledge that the idea of cause asks to com-firm it something quite independent of experience, that is abstract. But such examples are common. We never saw two objects continue to approach without meeting; but we are constrained to believe that lines of certain descriptions can forever approach and never meet.

The uniformity of sequence is, in fact, in the physical sciences never assumed to express the relation of cause and effect, until the connection between the antecedent and consequent can be set forth abstractly in mathematical formulæ. The sequence of the planetary motions was discovered by Kepler, but it was reserved for Newton to prove the theoretical necessity of this motion and establish its mathematical relations. The sequence of sensations to impressions is well known, but the law of the sequence remains the desideratum in psychology.[1]

Science, therefore, has been correctly defined as "the knowledge of system." Its aim is to ascertain the laws of phenomena, to define the "order in things." Its fundamental postulate is that order exists, that all things are "lapped in universal law." It acknowledges no exception, and it considers that all law is capable of final expression in quantity, in mathematical symbols.

---

[1] This distinction is well set forth by A. von Humboldt, *Kosmos*, p. 388 (Phila., 1869).

It is the manifest of reason, "whose unceasing endeavor is to banish the idea of Chance."[1]

We thus see that its postulate is the same as that of the religious sentiment. Wherein then do they differ? Not in the recognition of chance. Accident, chance, does not exist for the religious sense in any stage of its growth. Everywhere religion proclaims in the words of Dante:—

> "le cose tutte quante,
> Hann' ordine tra loro;"

everywhere in the more optimistic faiths it holds this order, in the words of St. Augustine, to be one "most fair, of excellent things."[2]

What we call "the element of chance" is in its scientific sense that of which we do not know the law; while to the untutored religious mind it is the manifestation of divine will. The Kamschatkan, when his boat is lost in the storm, attributes it to the vengeance of a god angered because he scraped the snow from his shoes with a knife, instead of using a piece of wood; if a Dakota has bad luck in hunting, he says it is caused by his wife stepping over a bone and

---

[1] "Ueberall den Zufall zu verbannen, zu verhindern, dass in dem Gebiete des Beobachtens und Denkens er nicht zu herrschen scheine, im Gebiete des Handelns nicht herrsche, ist das Streben der Vernunft." Wilhelm von Humboldt, *Ueber Goethe's Hermann und Dorothea*, iv.

[2] "Iste ordo pulcherrimus rerum valde bonarum." *Confessiones*, Lib. xiii. cap. xxxv.

thus irritating a spirit. The idea of cause, the sentiment of order, is as strong as ever, but it differs from that admitted by science in recognizing as a possible efficient motor that which is incapable of mathematical expression, namely, a volition, a will. *Voluntas Dei asylum ignorantiæ*, is no unkind description of such an opinion.

So long as this recognition is essential to the life of a religious system, just so long it will and must be in conflict with science, with every prospect of the latter gaining the victory. Is the belief in volition as an efficient cause indispensable to the religious sentiment in general? For this vital question we are not yet prepared, but must first consider the remaining rational postulates it assumes. The second is

II. This order is one of intelligence.

By this is not meant that the order is one of *an* Intelligence, but simply that the order which exists in things is conformable to man's thinking power,—that if he knows the course of events he can appreciate their relations,—that facts can be subsumed under thoughts. Whatever scheme of order there were, would be nothing to him unless it were conformable to his intellectual functions. It could not form the matter of his thought.[1]

[1] "The notion of a God is not contained in the mere notion

Science, which deals in the first instance exclusively with phenomena, also assumes this postulate. It recognizes that when the formal laws, which it is its mission to define, are examined apart from their material expression, when they are emptied of their phenomenal contents, they show themselves to be logical constructions, reasoned truths, in other words, forms of intelligence. The votary who assumes the order one of volition alone, or volition with physical necessity, still assumes the volitions are as comprehensible as are his own; that they are purposive; that the order, even if not clear to him, is both real and reasonable. Were it not so, did he believe that the gods carried out their schemes through a series of caprices inconceivable to intelligence, through absolute chance, insane caprice, or blind fate, he could neither see in occurrences the signs of divine rule, nor hope for aid in obtaining his wishes. In fact, order is only conceivable to man at all as an order conformable to his own intelligence.

This second postulate embraces what has been recently called the "Principle of continuity," indispensable to sane thought of any kind. A late work defines it as " the trust that the Supreme Governor of the Universe will not

of Cause, that is the notion of Fate or Power. To this must be added Intelligence," etc. Sir Wm. Hamilton, *Lectures on Metaphysics*, Lecture ii.

put us to permanent intellectual confusion."[1] Looked at closely, it is the identification of order with reason.

The third and final postulate of the religious sentiment is that

III. All intelligence is one in kind.

Religion demands that there be a truth which is absolutely true, and that there be a goodness which is universally and eternally good. Each system claims the possession, and generally the exclusive possession, of this goodness and truth. They are right in maintaining these views, for unless such is the case, unless there is an absolute truth, cognizable to man, yet not transcended by any divine intelligence, all possible religion becomes mere child's play, and its professed interpretation of mysteries but trickery.

The Grecian sophists used to meet the demonstrations of the mathematicians and philosophers by conceding that they did indeed set forth the truth, so far as man's intelligence goes, but that to the intelligence of other beings—a bat or an angel, for example—they might not hold good at all; that there is a different truth for different intelligences ; that the intelligence makes the truth; and that as for the absolutely true, true to every intelligence, there is no such thing. They acknowledged that a simple syl-

[1] *The Unseen Universe*, p. 60.

logism, constructed on these premises, made their own assertions partake of the doubtful character that was by them ascribed to other human knowledge. But this they gracefully accepted as the inevitable conclusion of reasoning. Their position is defended to-day by the advocates of "positivism," who maintain the relativity of all truth.

But such a conclusion is wholly incompatible with the religious mind. It must assume that there are some common truths, true infinitely, and therefore, that in all intelligence there is an essential unity of kind. "This postulation," says a close thinker, "is the very foundation and essence of religion. Destroy it, and you destroy the very possibility of religion." [1]

Clear as this would seem to be to any reflective mind, yet, strange to say, it is to-day the current fashion for religious teachers to deny it. Scared by a phantasm of their own creation, they have deserted the only position in which it is possible to defend religion at all. Afraid of the accusation that they

---

[1] James Frederick Ferrier, *Lectures on Greek Philosophy*, p. 13 (Edinburgh, 1866). On a question growing directly out of this, to wit, the relative character of good and evil, Mr. J. S. Mill expresses himself thus: "My opinion of this doctrine is, that it is beyond all others which now engage speculative minds, the decisive one between moral good and evil for the Christian world." *Examination of Hamilton's Philosophy*, p. 90.

make God like man, they have removed Him beyond the pale of all intelligence, and logically, therefore, annihilated every conception of Him.

Teachers and preachers do not tire of telling their followers that God is incomprehensible; that his ways are past finding out; that he is the Unconditioned, the Infinite, the Unknowable. They really mean that he is another order of intelligence, which, to quote a famous comparison of Spinoza, has the same name as ours, but is no more one with it than the dog is one with his namesake, the dog-star!

They are eagerly seconded in this position by a school of writers who distinctly see where such a doctrine leads, and who do not hesitate to carry it home. Mr. Mill is right in his scorn for those who " erect the incurable limitations of the human conceptive faculty into laws of the outward universe," if there are such limitations. And Mr. Spencer is justified in condemning " the transcendent audacity which passes current as piety," if his definition of the underlying verity of religion is admitted—that it is " the consciousness of an inscrutable power which, in its nature, transcends intuition, and is beyond imagination."[1] They are but following the orthodox Sir William Hamilton, who says: " Creation must be thought as the incomprehen-

[1] *First Principles*, pp. 108, 127.

sible evolution of power into energy."[1] We are to think that which by the terms of the proposition is unthinkable! A most wise master!

Let it be noted that the expressions such as inscrutable, incomprehensible, unknowable, etc., which such writers use, are avowedly not limited to man's intelligence in its present state of cultivation, but are applied to his *kind* of intelligence, no matter how far trained. They mean that the inscrutable, etc., is not merely not *at present* open to man's observation—that were a truism—but that it cannot be subsumed under the laws of his reasoning powers. In other words, they deny that all intelligence is one in *kind*. Some accept this fully, and concede that what are called the laws of order, as shown by science, are only matters of experience, true here and now, not necessarily and absolutely true.

This is a consistent inference, and applies, of course, with equal force to all moral laws and religious dogmas.

The arguments brought against such opinions have been various. The old reply to the sophists has been dressed in modern garb, and it has been repeatedly put that if no statement is really true, then this one, to wit " no statement is really true," also is not true ; and if that is the

[1] *Lectures on Metaphysics,* Vol. I., p. 690.

case, then there are statements which really are true. The theory of evolution as a dogma has been attacked by its own maxims; in asserting that all knowledge is imperfect, it calls its own verity into question. If all truth is relative, then this at least is absolutely true.

It has also been noted that all such words as incomprehensible, unconditioned, infinite, unknowable, are in their nature privatives, they are not a thought but are only one element of a thought. As has been shown in the first chapter, every thought is made up of a positive and a privative, and it is absurd and unnatural to separate the one from the other. The concept man, regarded as a division of the higher concept animal, is made up of man and not-man. In so far as other animals are included under the term "not-man" they do not come into intelligent cognition; but that does not mean that they cannot do so. So "the unconditioned" is really a part of the thought of "the conditioned," the "unknowable" a part of the "knowable," the "infinite" a part of the thought of the "finite." Under material images these privatives, as such, cannot be expressed; but in pure thought which deals with symbols and types alone, they can be.

But if the abstract laws of thought themselves are confined in the limits of one kind of intelligence, then we cannot take an appeal to them to attack this sophism. Therefore on maintaining their integrity the discussion must finally rest. This has been fully recognized by thinkers, one of whom has not long since earnestly called attention to " the urgent necessity of fathoming the psychical mechanism on which rests all our intellectual life." [1]

In this endeavor the attempt has been made to show that the logical laws are derived in accordance with the general theory of evolution from the natural or material laws of thinking. These, as I have previously remarked, are those of the association of ideas, and come under the general heads of contiguity and similarity. Such combinations are independent of the aim of the logical laws, which is *correct* thinking. A German writer, Dr. Windelband, has therefore argued that as experience, strengthened by hereditary transmission, continued to show that the particular combinations which are in accord with what we call the laws of thought furnished the best, that is, the most useful results, they were adopted in preference to others and finally assumed as the criteria of truth.

Of course it follows from this that as these laws are merely the outcome of human experience they can have no validity outside of it. Consequently, adds the writer I have quoted, just as the study of optics teaches us that the human eye yields a very different picture of the exter-

[1] Professor Steinthal in the *Zeitschrift für Völkerpsychologie*.

nal world from that given by the eye of a fly, for instance, and as each of them is equally far from the reality, so the truth which our intelligence enables us to reach is not less remote from that which is the absolutely true. He considers that this is proven by the very nature of the " law of contradiction " itself, which must be inconsistent with the character of absolute thought. For in the latter, positive truth only can exist, therefore no negation, and no law about the relation of affirmative to negative.[1]

The latter criticism assumes that negation is of the nature of error, a mistake drawn from the use of the negative in applied logic. For in formal logic, whether as quantity or quality, that is, in pure mathematics or abstract thought, the reasoning is just as correct when negatives are employed as when positives, as I have remarked before. The other criticism is more important, for if we can reach the conclusion that the real laws of the universe are other than as we understand them, then our intelligence is not of a kind to represent them.

Such an opinion can be refuted directly. The laws which we profess to know are as operative in the remotest nebulae as in the planet we inhabit. It is altogether likely that countless

---

[1] Dr. W. Windelband, *Die Erkenntnisslehre unter dem voelkerpsychologischem Gesichtspunkte*, in the *Zeitschrift für Völkerpsychologie*, 1874, *Bd. VIII.* S. 165 *sqq.*

forms of intelligent beings inhabit the starry wastes, receiving through sensory apparatus widely different from ours very diverse impressions of the external world. All this we know, but we also know that if those beings have defined the laws which underlie phenomena, they have found them to be the same that we have; for were they in the least different, in principle or application, they could not furnish the means, as those we know do, of predicting the recurrence of the celestial motions with unfailing accuracy. Therefore the demonstrations of pure mathematics, such as the relation of an absciss to an ordinate, or of the diameter to the circumference, must be universally true; and hence the logical laws which are the ultimate criteria of these truths must also be true to every intelligence, real or possible.[1]

Another and forcible reply to these objections is that the laws which our intelligence has reached and recognizes as universally true are not only not derived from experience, but are in direct opposition to and are constantly contradicted by it. Neither sense nor imagination has ever portrayed a perfect circle in which the diameter bore to the circumference the exact proportion which we know it does bear. The very fact that we have

---

[1] I would ask the reader willing to pursue this reasoning further, to peruse the charming essay of Oersted, entitled *Das ganze Dasein Ein Vernunftreich.*

learned that our senses are wholly untrustworthy, and that experience is always fallacious, shows that we have tests of truth depending on some other faculty. "Each series of connected facts in nature furnishes the intimation of an order more exact than that which it directly manifests."[1]

But, it has been urged, granted that we have reached something like positive knowledge of those laws which are the *order* of the manifestation of phenomena, the real Inscrutable, the mysterious Unknowable, escapes us still; this is the *nature* of phenomenal manifestation, "the secret of the Power manifested in Existence."[2] At this point the physicist trips and falls; and here, too, the metaphysician stumbles.

I have already spoken of our aptitude to be frightened by a chimera, and deceived by such words as "nature" and "cause." Laws and rules, by which we express Order, are restrictive only in a condition of intelligence short of com-

[1] Geo. Boole, *An Investigation of the Laws of Thought*, p. 407.
[2] Herbert Spencer, *First Principles*, p. 112. Spinoza's famous proposition, previously quoted, *Unaquæque res quantum in se est, in suo esse perseverare conatur*, (*Ethices, Pars III., Prop. VI.,*) expresses also the ultimate of modern investigation. A recent critic considers it is a fallacy because the conatus "surreptitiously implies a sense of effort or struggle for existence," whereas the logical concept of a res does not involve effort (S. N. Hodgson, *The Theory of Practice*, vol. I. pp. 134-6, London, 1870.) The answer is that identity implies continuance. In organic life we have the fact of nutrition, a function whose duty is to supply waste, and hence offer direct opposition to perturbing forces.

pleteness, only therefore in that province of thought which concerns itself with material facts. The musician is not fettered by the laws of harmony, but only by those of discord. The truly virtuous man, remarks Aristotle, never has occasion to practise self-denial. Hence, mathematically, "the theory of the intellectual action involves the recognition of a sphere of thought from which all limits are withdrawn."[1] True freedom, real being, is only possible when law as such is inexistent. Only the lawless makes the law. When the idea of the laws of order thus disappears in that of free function consistent with perfect order, when, as Kant expresses it, we ascend from the contemplation of things acting according to law, to action according to the representation of law,[2] we can, without audacity, believe that we have penetrated the secret of existence, that we have reached the limits of explanation and found one wholly satisfying the highest reason. Intelligence, not apart from phenomena, but parallel with them, not under law, but through perfect harmony above it, *power one with being*, the will which is "the essence of reason," the emanant cause of phenomena, immanent only by the number of its relations we have not learned, this is the satisfying and exhaustive solution.

[1] Geo. Boole, *The Laws of Thought*, p. 419.
[2] Kant, *The Metaphysic of Ethics*, p. 23 (Eng. Trans. London, 1869.)

The folly lies not in claiming reason as the absolute, but in assuming that the absolute is beyond and against reason.

There is nothing new in this explanation; and it is none the worse for being old. If Anaxagoras discerned it dimly, and many a one since him has spoken of Intelligence, Reason, Nous or Logos as the constructive factor of the creation; if "all the riper religions of the Orient assumed as their fundamental principle that unless the Highest penetrates all parts of the Universe, and itself conditions whatever is conditioned, no universal order, no Kosmos, no real existence is thinkable;"[1] such inadequate expressions should never obscure the truth that reason in its loftiest flights descries nothing nobler than itself.

The relative, as its name implies, for ever presupposes and points to the absolute, the latter an Intelligence also, not one that renders ours futile and fallacious, but one that imparts to ours the capacity we possess of reaching eternal and ubiquitous truth. The severest mathematical reasoning forces us to this conclusion, and we can dispense with speculation about it.

Only on the principle which here receives its proof, that man has something in him of God, that the norm of the true holds good throughout,

---

[1] Creuzer, *Symbolik und Mythologie der alten Voelker*, Bd. I. s. 291.

can he know or care anything about divinity. "It takes a god to discern a god," profoundly wrote Novalis.

When a religion teaches what reason disclaims, not through lack of testimony but through a denial of the rights of reason, then that religion wars against itself and will fall. Faith is not the acceptance of what intelligence rejects, but a suspension of judgment for want of evidence. A thoroughly religious mind will rejoice when its faith is shaken with doubt; for the doubt indicates increased light rendering perceptible some possible error not before seen.

Least of all should a believer in a divine revelation deny the oneness of intelligence. For if he is right, then the revealed truth he talks about is but relative and partial, and those inspired men who claimed for it the sign manual of the Absolute were fools, insane or liars.

If the various arguments I have rehearsed indicate conclusively that in the laws of thought we have the norms of absolute truth—and skepticism on this point can be skepticism and not belief only by virtue of the very law which it doubts—some important corollaries present themselves.

Regarding in the first place the nature of these laws, we find them very different from those of physical necessity — those which are called the laws of nature. The latter are authoritative, they are never means to an end, they admit no exception, they leave no room for error. Not so with the laws of reasoning. Man far more frequently disregards than obeys them; they leave a wide field for fallacy. Wherein then lies that theoretical necessity which is the essence of law? The answer is that the laws of reasoning are *purposive* only, they are regulative, not constitutive, and their theoretical necessity. lies in the end, the result of reasoning, that is, in the knowing, in the recognition of truth. They are what the Germans call *Zweckgesetze*.[1]

But in mathematical reasoning and in the processes of physical nature the absolute character of the laws which prevail depends for its final necessity on their consistency, their entire correspondence with the laws of right reasoning. Applied to them the purposive character of the laws is not seen, for their ends are fulfilled. We are brought, therefore, to the momentous conclusion that the manifestation of Order, whether in material or mental processes, " affords a presumption, not measurable indeed but real, of the fulfilment of an end or purpose;"[1] and this purpose, one which has other objects in view than the continuance of physical processes. The history of mind, from protoplasmic sensation

[1] See this distinction between physical and thought laws fully set forth by Prof. Boole in the appendix to *The Laws of Thought*, and by Dr. Windelband, *Zeitschrift für Voelkerpsychologie*. Bd. VIII., s. 165 sqq.

[2] Geo. Boole, u. s. p. 399.

upward, must be a progression, whose end will be worth more than was its beginning, a process, which has for its purpose the satisfaction of the laws of mind. This is nothing else than correct thinking, the attainment of truth.

But this conclusion, reached by a searching criticism of the validity of scientific laws, is precisely that which is the postulate of all developed creeds. "The faith of all historical religions," says Bunsen, "starts from the assumption of a universal moral order, in which the good is alone the true, and the true is the only good."[1]

The purposive nature of the processes of thought, as well as the manner in which they govern the mind, is illustrated by the history of man. His actions, whether as an individual or as a nation, are guided by ideas not derived from the outer world, for they do not correspond to actual objects, but from mental pictures of things as he wants them to exist. These are his hopes, his wishes, his ideals; they are the more potent, and prompt to more vigorous action, the clearer they are to his mind. Even when he is unconscious of them, they exist as tendencies, or instincts, inherited often from some remote ancestor, perhaps even the heir-loom of a stage of

[1] "Der Glaube aller geschichtlichen Religionen geht aus von dieser Annahme einer sittlichen, in Gott bewusst lebenden, Weltordnung, wonach das Gute das allein Wahre ist, and das Wahre das allein Gute." *Gott in der Geschichte*, Bd. I. s. xl. Leipzig, 1857.

lower life, for they occur where sensation alone is present, and are an important factor in general evolution.

It is usually conceded that this theory of organic development very much attenuates the evidence of what is known as the argument from design in nature, by which the existence of an intelligent Creator is sought to be shown. If the distinction between the formal laws of mathematics, which are those of nature, and logic, which are those of mind, be fully understood, no one will seek such an argument in the former but in the latter only, for they alone, as I have shown, are purposive, and they are wholly so. The only God that nature points to is an adamantine Fate.

If religion has indeed the object which Bunsen assigns it, physical phenomena cannot concern it. Its votaries should not look to change the operation of natural laws by incantations, prayers or miracles.

Whenever in the material world there presents itself a seeming confusion, it is certain to turn out but an incompleteness of our observation, and on closer inspection it resolves itself into some higher scheme of Order. This is not so in the realm of thought. Wrong thinking never can become right thinking. A profound writer has said: " One explanation only of these facts can be given, viz., that the distinction between *true* and *false*, between *correct* and *incorrect*, exists in the processes of the intellect, but not in the region of a physical necessity."[1] A religion therefore which claims as its mission the discovery of the true and its identification with the good,—in other words the persuading man that he should always act in accordance with the dictates of right reasoning—should be addressed primarily to the intellect.

As man can attain to certain truths which are without any mixture of fallacy, which when once he comprehends them he can never any more doubt, and which though thus absolute do not fetter his intellect but first give it the use of all its powers to the extent of those truths; so he can conceive of an Intelligence in which all truth is thus without taint of error. Not only is such an Intelligence conceivable, it is necessary to conceive it, in order to complete the scientific induction of " a sphere of thought from which all limits are withdrawn," forced upon us by the demonstrations of the exact sciences.[2]

Thus do we reach the foundation for the faith in a moral government of the world, which it has been the uniform characteristic of religions to

---

[1] Geo Boole, *Laws of Thought*, p. 410.

[2] The latest researches in natural science confirm the expressions of W. von Humboldt: "Das Streben der Natur ist auf etwas Unbeschränktes gerichtet." " Die Natur mit endlichen Mitteln unendliche Zwecke verfolgt." *Ueber den Geschlechtsunterschied, etc.*

assert; but a government, as thus analytically reached, not easily corresponding with that which popular religion speaks of. Such feeble sentiments as mercy, benevolence and effusive love, scarcely find place in this conception of the source of universal order. In this cosmical dust-cloud we inhabit, whose each speck is a sun, man's destiny plays a microscopic part. The vexed question whether ours is the best possible or the worst possible world, drops into startling insignificance. Religion has taught the abnegation of self; science is first to teach the humiliation of the race. Not for man's behoof were created the greater and the lesser lights, not for his deeds will the sun grow dark or the stars fall, not with any reference to his pains or pleasure was this universe spread upon the night. That Intelligence which pursues its own ends in this All, which sees from first to last the chain of causes which mould human action, measures not its purposes by man's halting sensations. Such an Intelligence is fitly described by the philosopher-poet as one,

"Wo die Gerechtigkeit so Wurzel schläget,
Und Schuld und Unschuld so erhaben wäget
Dass sie vertritt die Stelle aller Güte." [1]

In the scheme of the universe, pain and pleasure, truth and error, has each its fitness, and no single thought or act can be judged

[1] Wilhelm von Humboldt, *Sonnette*, "Höchste Gerechtigkeit."

apart from all others that ever have been and ever shall be.

Such was the power that was contemplated by the Hebrew prophet, one from which all evil things and all good things come, and who disposes them all to the fulfilment of a final purpose:

"I am the Lord and there is none else. I form the light and create darkness; I make peace and create evil."

"I am God and there is none like me, declaring the end from the beginning, and from ancient times the things which are not yet done." [1]

In a similar strain the ancient Aryan sang:—

"This do I ask thee, tell me, O Ahura!
Who is he, working good, made the light and also darkness?
Who is he, working good, made the sleep as well as waking?
Who the night, as well as noon and the morning?"

And the reply came:

"Know also this, O pure Zarathustra: through my wisdom, through which was the beginning of the world, so also its end shall be." [2]

Or as the Arabian apostle wrote, inspired by the same idea:—

"Praise the name of thy Lord, the Most High,
Who hath created and balanced all things,
Who hath fixed their destinies and guideth them."

"The Revelation of this book is from the Mighty, the Wise. We have not created the Heavens and the Earth and all that is between them otherwise than with a purpose and for a settled term." [3]

---

[1] Isaiah, xlv. 7; xlvi. 10.
[2] *Khordah—avesta, Ormazd—Yasht*, 38, and *Yaçna*, 42.
[3] *The Koran*, Suras lxxxvii., xlvi.

THE PRAYER AND ITS ANSWER.

SUMMARY.

Religion starts with a Prayer. This is an appeal to the unknown, and is indispensable in religious thought. The apparent exceptions of Buddhism and Confucianism.

All prayers relate to the fulfilment of a wish. At first its direct object is alone thought of. This so frequently fails that the indirect object rises into view. This stated to be the increase of the pleasurable emotions. The inadequacy of this statement.

The answers to prayer. As a form of Expectant Attention, it exerts much subjective power. Can it influence external phenomena? It is possible. Deeply religious minds reject both these answers, however. They claim the objective answer to be Inspiration. All religions unite in this claim.

Inspirations have been contradictory. That is genuine which teaches truths which cannot be doubted concerning duty and deity. A certain mental condition favors the attainment of such truths. This simulated in religious enthensm. Examples. It is allied to the most intense intellectual action, but its steps remain unknown.

CHAPTER IV.

THE PRAYER AND ITS ANSWER.

THE foregoing analysis of the religious sentiment results in finding it, even in its simplest forms, a product of complicated reasoning forced into action by some of the strongest emotions, and maintaining its position indefeasibly through the limitations of the intellect. This it does, however, with a certain nobleness, for while it wraps the unknown in sacred mystery, it proclaims man one in nature with the Highest, by birthright a son of the gods, of an intelligence akin to theirs, and less than they only in degree. Through thus presenting at once his strength and his feebleness, his grandeur and his degradation, religion goes beyond philosophy or utility in suggesting motives for exertion, stimuli to labor. This phase of it will now occupy us.

The Religious Sentiment manifests itself in thought, in word and in act through the respective media of the Prayer, the Myth and the Cult. The first embraces the personal relations of the individual to the object of his worship, the second expresses the opinions current in a community about the nature and actions of that object, the last includes the symbols and ceremonies under and by which it is represented and propitiated.

The first has the logical priority. Man cares nothing for God — *can* care nothing for him practically—except as an aid to the fulfilment of his desires, the satisfaction of his wants, as the " ground of his hopes." The root of the religious sentiment, I have said, is " a wish whose fruition depends upon unknown power." An appeal for aid to this unknown power, is the first form of prayer in its religious sense. It is not merely " the soul's sincere desire." This may well be and well directed, and yet not religious, as the devotion of the mathematician to the solution of an important problem. With the desire must be the earnest appeal to the unknown. A theological dictionary I have at hand almost correctly defines it as " a petition for spiritual or physical benefits which [we believe] we cannot obtain without divine co-operation." The words in brackets must be inserted to complete the definition.

It need not be expressed in language. Rousseau, in his *Confessions*, tells of a bishop who, in visiting his diocese, came across an old woman who was troubled because she could frame no prayer in words, but only cry, "Oh!" "Good mother," said the wise bishop, "Pray always so. Your prayers are better than ours."[1]

A petition for assistance is, as I have said, one of its first forms; but not its only one. The assistance asked in simple prayers is often nothing more than the neutrality of the gods, their non-interference; "no preventing Providence," as the expression is in our popular religion. Prayers of fear are of this kind:

"And they say, God be merciful,
Who ne'er said, God be praised."

Some of the Egyptian formulæ even threaten the gods if they prevent success.[2] The wish accomplished, the prayer may be one of gratitude, often enough of that kind described by La Rochefoucauld, of which a prominent element is "a lively sense of possible favors to come."[3]

Or again, self-abasement being so natural a form of flattery that to call ourselves "obedient

[1] The "silent worship" of the Quakers is defended by the writers of that sect, on the ground that prayer is "often very imperfectly performed and sometimes materially interrupted by the use of words." Joseph John Gurney, *The Distinguishing Views and Practice of the Society of Friends*, p. 300. (London, 1834.)

[2] Creuzer, *Symbolik und Mythologie der alten Völker*, Bd. I., s. 162.

[3] The learned Bishop Butler, author of the *Analogy of Religion*, justly gives prominence to "our expectation of future benefits," as a reason for gratitude to God. *Sermons*, p. 155. (London, 1841.)

and humble servants" of others, has passed into one of the commonest forms of address, many prayers are made up of similar expressions of humility and contrition, the votary calling himself a "miserable sinner" and a "vile worm," and on the other hand magnifying his Lord as greater than all other gods, mighty and helpful to those who assiduously worship him.

In some form or other, as of petition, gratitude or contrition, uttered in words or confined to the aspirations of the soul, prayer is a necessary factor in the religious life. It always has been, and it must be present.

The exceptions which may be taken to this in religious systems are chiefly two, those supposed to have been founded by Buddha Sakyamuni and Confucius.

It is undoubtedly correct that Buddha discouraged prayer. He permitted it at best in the inferior grades of discipleship. For himself, and all who reached his stage of culture, he pronounced it futile.

But Buddha did not set out to teach a religion, but rather the inutility of all creeds. He struck shrewdly at the root of them by placing the highest condition of man in the total extinguishment of desire. He bound the gods in fetters by establishing a theory of causal connection (the twelve Nidana) which does away with the necessity of ruling powers. He then swept both matter and spirit into unreality by establishing the canon of ignorance, that the highest knowledge is to know that nothing is; that there is neither being nor not-being, nor yet the becoming. After this wholesale iconoclasm the only possible object in life for the sage is the negative one of avoiding pain, which though as unreal as anything else, interferes with his meditations on its unreality. To this negative end the only aid he can expect is from other sages who have gone farther in self-cultivation. Self, therefore, is the first, the collective body of sages is the second, and the written instruction of Buddha is the third; and these three are the only sources to which the consistent Buddhist looks for aid.

This was Buddha's teaching. But it is not Buddhism as professed by the hundreds of millions in Ceylon, in Thibet, China, Japan, and Siberia, who claim Sakyamuni under his names Buddha, the awakened, Tathagata, thus gone, or gone before, Siddartha, the accomplisher of the wish, and threescore and ten others of like purport, as their inspired teacher. Millions of saints, holy men, Buddhas, they believe, are ready to aid in every way the true believer, and incessant, constant prayer is, they maintain, the one efficient means to insure this aid. Repetition, dinning the divinities and wearying them into answering, is their theory. Therefore they will repeat a short formula of four words (*om mani padme hum*—Om! the jewel in the lotus, amen) thousands of times a day; or, as they correctly think it not a whit more mechanical, they write it a million times on strips of paper, fasten it around a cylinder, attach this to a water or a wind-wheel, and thus sleeping or waking, at home or abroad, keep up a steady fire of prayer at the gods, which finally, they sanguinely hope, will bring them to submission.

No sect has such entire confidence in the power of prayer as the Buddhists. The most pious Mahometan or Christian does not approach their faith. After all is said and done, the latter has room to doubt the efficacy of his prayer. It may be refused. Not so the Buddhists. They have a syllogism which covers the case completely, as follows:—

> All things are in the power of the gods.
> The gods are in the power of prayer.
> Prayer is at the will of the saint.
> Therefore all things are in the power of the saint.

The only reason that any prayer fails is that it is not repeated often enough—a statement difficult to refute.

The case with Confucius was different.[1] No speculative dreamer, but a practical man, bent

---

[1] The expressions of Confucius' religious views may be found in *The Doctrine of the Mean*, chaps. xiii., xvi., the *Analects*, i., 99, 100, vii., and in a few other passages of the canonical books.

on improving his fellows by teaching them self-reliance, industry, honesty, good feeling and the attainment of material comfort, he did not see in the religious systems and doctrines of his time any assistance to these ends. Therefore, like Socrates and many other men of ancient and modern times, without actually condemning the faiths around him, or absolutely neglecting some external respect to their usages, he taught his followers to turn away from religious topics and occupy themselves with subjects of immediate utility. For questions of duty, man, he taught, has a sufficient guide within himself. "What you do not like," he said, "when done to yourself, do not to others." The wishes, he adds, should be limited to the attainable; thus their disappointment can be avoided by a just estimate of one's own powers. He used to compare a wise man to an archer: "When the archer misses the target, he seeks for the cause of his failure within himself." He did not like to talk about spiritual beings. When asked whether the dead had knowledge, he replied: "There is no present urgency about the matter. If they have, you will know it for yourself in time." He did not deny the existence of unseen powers; on the contrary, he said: "The *kwei shin* (the most general term for supernatural beings) enter into all things, and there is nothing without them;" but he added, "We look for them and do not see them; we listen, but do not hear them." In speaking of deity, he dropped the personal syllable (*te*) and only spoke of heaven, in the indefinite sense. Such was this extraordinary man. The utilitarian theory, what we call the common sense view of life, was never better taught. But his doctrine is not a religion. His followers erect temples, and from filial respect pay the usual honors to their ancestors, as Confucius himself did. But they ignore religious observances, strictly so-called.

These examples, therefore, do not at all conflict with the general statement that no religion can exist without prayer. On the contrary, it is the native expression of the religious sentiment, that to which we must look for its most hidden meaning. The thoughtful Novalis, whose meditations are so rich in reflections on the religious nature of man, well said: " Prayer is to religion what thought is to philosophy. To pray is to make religion. The religious sense prays with like necessity that the reason thinks."

Whatever the form of the prayer, it has direct or indirect relation to the accomplishment of a wish. David prays to the Lord as the one who " satisfies the desire of every living thing," who " will fulfil the desire of them that fear him," and it is with the like faith that the heart of every votary is stirred when he approaches in prayer the divinity he adores.

Widely various are the things wished for. Their character is the test of religions. In primitive faiths and in uncultivated minds, prayers are confined to the nearest material advantages; they are directed to the attainment of food, of victory in combat, of safety in danger, of personal prosperity. They may all be summed up in a line of one which occurs in the Rig Veda: " O Lord Varuna! Grant that we may prosper in *getting and keeping!*"

Beyond this point of "getting and keeping," few primitive prayers take us. Those of the American Indians, as I have elsewhere shown, remained in this stage among the savage tribes, and rose above it only in the civilized states of Mexico and Peru. Prayers for health, for plenteous harvests, for safe voyages and the like are of this nature, though from their familiarity to us they seem less crude than the simple-hearted petition of the old Aryan, which I have quoted. They mean the same.

The more thoughtful votaries of the higher forms of religion have, however, frequently drawn the distinction between the direct and indirect fulfilment of the wish. An abundant harvest, restoration to health, or a victory in battle is the object of our hopes, not in itself, but for its results upon ourselves. These, in their final expression, can mean nothing else than agreeable sensations and pleasurable emotions.

These, therefore, are the real though indirect objects of such prayers; often unconsciously so, because the ordinary devotee has little capacity and less inclination to analyze the nature of his religious feelings.

A recent writer, Mr. Hodgson, has said: "The real answer to prayer is the increase of the joyful emotions, the decrease of the painful ones."[1] It would seem a simpler plan to make this directly the purport of our petitions; but to the modern mind this naked simplicity would be distasteful.

Nor is the ordinary supplicant willing to look so far. The direct, not the indirect object of the wish, is what he wants. The lazzarone of Naples prays to his patron saint to favor his choice of a lottery ticket; if it turn out an unlucky number he will take the little leaden image of the saint from his pocket, revile it, spit on it, and trample it in the mud. Another man, when his prayer for success is not followed by victory, sends gifts to the church, flogs himself in public and fasts. Xenophon gives us in his *Economics* the prayer of a pious Athenian of his time, in the person of Ischomachus. "I seek to obtain," says the latter, " from the gods by just prayers, strength and health, the respect of the community, the love of my friends, an honorable termination to my combats, and riches, the fruit of honest in-

[1] *An Inquiry into the Theory of Practice*, p. 330.

dustry." Xenophon evidently considered these appropriate objects for prayer, and from the petitions in many recent manuals of devotion, I should suppose most Christians of to-day would not see in them anything inappropriate.

In spite of the effort that has been made by Professor Creuzer[1] to show that the classical nations rose to a higher use of prayer, one which made spiritual growth in the better sense of the phrase its main end; I think such instances were confined to single philosophers and poets. They do not represent the prayers of the average votary. Then and now he, as a rule, has little or no idea of any other answer to his prayer than the attainment of his wish.

As such petitions, however, more frequently fail than succeed in their direct object, and as the alternative of considering them impotent is not open to the votary, some other explanation of their failure was taught in very early days. At first, it was that the god was angered, and refused the petition out of revenge. Later, the indirect purpose of such a prayer asserted itself

---

[1] *Symbolik und Mythologie der Alten Völker.* Bd. I., ss. 165, sqq. One of the most favorable examples (not mentioned by Creuzer) is the formula with which Apollonius of Tyana closed every prayer and gave as the summary of all: "Give me, ye Gods, what I deserve"—Δοιητε μοι τα οφειλομενα. The Christian's comment on this would be in the words of Hamlet's reply to Polonius: "God's bodkin, man! use every man after his desert and who should 'scape whipping?"

more clearly, and aided by a nobler conception of Divinity, suggested that the refusal of the lower is a preparation for a higher reward. Children, in well-ordered households, are frequently refused by parents who love them well; this present analogy was early seized to explain the failure of prayer. Unquestioning submission to the divine will was inculcated. Some even went so far as to think it improper to define any wish at all, and subsumed all prayer under the one formula, "Thy will be done." Such was the teaching of St. Augustine, whose favorite prayer was *Da quod jubes, et jube quod vis*, a phrase much criticized by Pelagius and others of his time as too quietistic.[1] The usual Christian doctrine of resignation proceeds in theory to this extent. Such a notion of the purpose of prayer leads to a cheerful acceptance of the effects of physical laws, effects which an enlightened religious mind never asks to be altered in its favor, for the promises and aims of religion should be wholly outside the arena of their operation. The ideal prayer has quite other objects than to work material changes.

To say, as does Mr. Hodgson, that its aim is the increase of the joyful emotions is far from

[1] Aurelii Augustini, *De Dono Perseverantiæ*, cap. xx. Comte remarks " Depuis St. Augustin toutes les âmes pures ont de plus en plus senti, à travers l'égoisme Chrétien, que prier peut n'être pas demander." *Système de Politique Positive*, I., p. 260. Popular Protestantism has retrograded in this respect.

sufficient. The same may be said of most human effort, the effort to make money, for instance. The indirect object of money-making is also the increase of the agreeable feelings. The similarity of purpose might lead to a belief that the aims of religion and business are identical.

Before we can fully decide on what, in the specifically religious sense of the word, is the answer to prayer, we should inquire as a matter of fact what effect it actually exerts, and to do this we should understand what it is as a psychological process. The reply to this is that prayer, in its psychological definition, is a form of Expectant Attention. It is always urged by religious teachers that it must be very earnest and continuous to be successful. " Importunity is of the essence of successful prayer," says Canon Liddon in a recent sermon. In the New Testament it is likened to a constant knocking at a door; and by a curious parity of thought the Chinese character for prayer is composed of the signs for a spirit and an axe or hammer.[1] We must "keep hammering" as a colloquial phrase has it. Strong belief is also required. To pray with faith we must expect with confidence.

[1] Plath, *Die Religion und Cultus der alten Chineser*, s. 836. This author observes that the Chinese prayers are confined to temporal benefits only, and are all either prayers of petition or gratitude. Prayers of contrition are unknown.

Now that such a condition of expectant attention, prolonged and earnest, will have a very powerful subjective effect, no one acquainted with the functions of the human economy can doubt. "Any state of the body," observes the physiologist Müller, " expected with certain confidence is very prone to ensue." A pill of bread-crumbs, which the patient supposes to contain a powerful cathartic, will often produce copious evacuations. No one who studies the history of medicine can question that scrofulous swellings and ulcerations were cured by the royal touch, that paralytics have regained the use of their limbs by touching the relics of the saints, and that in many countries beside Judea the laying on of hands and the words of a holy man have made issues to heal and the lame to walk.[1]

Such effects are not disputed by physicians as probable results of prayer or faith considered as expectant attention. The stigmata of St. Francis d'Assisi are more than paralleled by those of Louise Lateau, now living at Bois d'Haine in Belgium, whose hands, feet and side bleed every Friday like those of Christ on the cross. A commission of medical men after the most careful precautions against deception attributed these hemorrhages to the effect of expectation

[1] Numerous examples can be found in medical text books, for instance in Dr. Tuke's, *The Influence of the Mind on the Body.* London, 1873.

(prayer) vastly increased in force by repetition.[1] If human testimony is worth anything, the cures of Porte Royale are not open to dispute.[2]

The mental consequences of a prayerful condition of mind are to inspire patience under afflictions, hope in adversity, courage in the presence of danger and a calm confidence in the face of death itself. How mightily such influences have worked in history is shown in every religious war, and in the lives of the martyrs of all faiths. It matters not what they believed, so only that they believed it thoroughly, and the gates of Hades could not prevail against them.

No one will question that these various and momentous results are the legitimate effects or answers to prayers. But whether prayer can influence the working of the material forces external to the individual is a disputed point. If it cannot in some way do this, prayers for rain, for harvests, for safety at sea, for restoration to health, for delivery from grasshoppers[3] and

[1] The commission appointed by the Royal Academy of Medicine of Belgium on Louise Lateau reported in March, 1875, and most of the medical periodicals of that year contain abstracts of its paper.

[2] They may be found in the life of Pascal, written by his sister, and in many other works of the time.

[3] It is worthy of note, as an exponent of the condition of religious thought in 1875, that in May of that year the Governor of the State of Missouri appointed by official proclamation a day of prayer to check the advance of the grasshoppers. He should also have requested the clergy to pronounce the ban of

pestilence, whether for our own benefit or others, are hardly worth reciting. A physicist expresses the one opinion in these words: " Science asserts that without a disturbance of natural law, quite as serious as the stoppage of an eclipse or the rolling of the St. Lawrence up the Falls of Niagara, no act of humiliation, individual or national, could call one shower from heaven or deflect toward us a single beam of the sun." " Assuming the efficacy of free prayer to produce changes in external nature, it necessarily follows that natural laws are more or less at the mercy of man's volition." [1]

This authoritative statement, much discussed at the time it was published, does not in fact express the assertion of science. To the scientific apprehension, man's volitions and his prayers are states of emotion, inseparably connected in their manifestations with changes in his cerebral structure, with relative elevation of temperature, and with the elimination of oxygen and phosphorus, in other words with chemico-vital phenomena and the transformation of force. Science also adds that there is a constant interaction of all force, and it is not prepared to deny that the force expended by a national or individual prayer may become a co-operating cause in

the Church against them, as the Bishop of Rheims did in the ninth century.

[1] Tyndall, *On Prayer and Natural Law*, 1872.

the material change asked for, even if the latter be a rain shower. This would not affect a natural law but only its operation, and that much every act of our life does. The fact that persistency and earnestness in prayer—*i. e.*, the increased development of force—add to its efficacy, would accord with such a scientific view. It would further be very materially corroborated by the accepted doctrine of the orders of force. A unit of electrical or magnetic force equals many of the force of gravity; a number of electrical units are required to make one of chemical force; and chemico-vital or "metabolic" force is still higher; whereas thought regarded as a form of force must be vastly beyond this again.

To render a loadstone, which lifts filings of iron by its magnetic force, capable of doing the same by the force of gravity, its density would have to be increased more than a thousand million times. All forces differ in like degree. Professor Faraday calculated that the force latent in the chemical composition of one drop of water, equals that manifested in an average thunderstorm. In our limited knowledge of the relation of forces therefore, a scientific man is rash to deny that the chemico-vital forces set loose by an earnest prayer may affect the operation of natural laws outside the body as they confessedly do in it.

Experience alone can decide such a question, and I for one, from theory and from observation, believe in the material efficacy of prayer. In a certain percentage of the cases where the wished-for material result followed, the physical force of the active cerebral action has seemed to me a co-operating cause. A physician can observe this to best advantage in the sickness of children, as they are free from subjective bias, their constitutions are delicately susceptible, and the prayers for them are in their immediate vicinity and very earnest.

But this admission after all is a barren one to the truly devout mind. The effect gained does not depend on the God to whom the prayer is offered. Blind physical laws bring it about, and any event that comes through their compulsive force is gelded of its power to fecundate the germs of the better religious life. The knowledge of this would paralyze faith.

Further to attenuate the value of my admission, another consideration arises, this time prompted not by speculative criticism, but by reverence itself. A scholar whom I have already quoted justly observes: "Whenever we prefer a request as a means of obtaining what we wish for, we are not praying in the religious sense of the term."[1] Or, as a recent theologian puts the same

[1] S. M. Hodgson, *An Inquiry into the Theory of Practice*, pp. 329, 330.

idea: "Every true prayer prays to be refused, if the granting of it would be hurtful to us or subversive of God's glory."[1] The real answer to prayer can never be an event or occurrence. Only in moments of spiritual weakness and obscured vision, when governed by his emotions or sensations, will the reverent soul ask a definite transaction, a modification in the operation of natural laws, still less such vulgar objects as victory, wealth or health.

The prayer of faith finds its only true objective answer in itself, in accepting whatever befalls as the revelation of the will of God as to what is best. This temper of mind as the real meaning of prayer was beautifully set forth by St. John: "If we know that he hear us, whatsoever we ask, we know that we have the petitions that we desired of him."[2]

But this solution of the problem does not go far enough. Prayer is claimed to have a positive effect on the mind other than resignation. Joyful emotions are its fruits, *spiritual enlightenment* its reward. These are more than cheerful acquiescence, nor can the latter come from objects of sense.

---

[1] The Rev. Dr. Thomas K. Conrad, *Thoughts on Prayer*, p. 54: New York, 1875.

[2] I. John, v. 15. "There are millions of prayers," says Richard Baxter, "that will all be found answered at death and judgment, which we know not to be answered any way but by believing it." *A Christian Directory*, Part II. chap. xxiii.

The most eminent teachers agree in banishing material pleasure and prosperity from holy desires. They are of one mind in warning against what the world and the flesh can offer, against the pursuit of riches, power and lust. Many counsel poverty and deliberate renunciation of all such things. Nor is the happiness they talk of that which the pursuit of intellectual truth brings. This, indeed, confers joy, of which whoever has tasted will not hastily return to the fleshpots of the senses, but it is easy to see that it is not religious. Prayer and veneration have not a part in it. Great joy is likewise given by the exercise of the imagination when stirred by art in some of its varied forms, and a joy more nearly allied to religion than is that of scientific investigation. But the esthetic emotions are well defined, and are distinctly apart from those concerned with the religious sentiment. Their most complete satisfaction rather excludes than encourages pious meditations. That which prayer ought to seek outside of itself is different from all of these, its dower must be divine.

We need not look long for it. Though hidden from the wise, it has ever been familiar to the unlearned. Man has never been in doubt as to what it is. He has been only too willing to believe he has received it.

In barbarism and civilization, in the old and

new worlds, the final answer to prayer has ever been acknowledged to be *inspiration*, revelation, the thought of God made clear to the mind of man, the mystical hypostasis through which the ideas of the human coincide with those of universal Intelligence. This is what the Pythian priestess, the Siberian shaman, the Roman sibyl, the Voluspan prophetess, the Indian medicine-man, all claimed in various degrees along with the Hebrew seers and the Mahometan teacher.[1]

The TRUTH, the last and absolute truth, is what is everywhere recognized as, if not the only, at least the completest, the highest answer to prayer. "Where I found the truth, there I found my God, himself the truth," says St. Augustine; and in a prayer by St. Chrysostom, the "Golden Mouth," unsurpassed in its grand simplicity, it is said: "Almighty Father, * * grant us in this world *knowledge of Thy truth*, and in the world to come, life everlasting." Never has the loftiest purpose of prayer been more completely stated. This it was that had been promised them by Him, to whom they looked as an Intercessor for their petitions, who had said: "I will send unto you the Comforter. * *

[1] " So wie das Gebet ein Hauptwurzel alter Lehre war, so war das Deuten und Offenbaren ihre ursprüngliche Form." Creuzer, *Symbolik und Mythologie der alten Völker*, Bd. I., s. 10. It were more accurate to say that divination is the answer to, rather than a form of prayer.

When he, the Spirit of Truth, is come, he will guide you unto all truth."

The belief that this answer is at all times attainable has always been recognized by the Christian Church, Apostolic, Catholic, and Protestant. Baptism was called by the Greek fathers, "enlightenment" (Φωτισμος), as by it the believer received the spirit of truth. The Romanist, in the dogma of infallibility, proclaims the perpetual inspiration of a living man; the Protestant Churches in many creeds and doctrinal works extend a substantial infallibility to all true believers, at least to the extent that they can be inspired to recognize, if not to receive divine verity.

The Gallican Confession of Faith, adopted in 1561, rests the principal evidence of the truth of the Scriptures on "*le témoignage et l'intérieure persuasion du Saint Esprit,*" and the Westminster Confession on "the inward work of the holy spirit." The Society of Friends maintain it as "a leading principle, that the work of the Holy Spirit in the soul is not only immediate and direct, but perceptible;" that it imparts truth "without any mixture of error;" and thus is something quite distinct from conscience, which is common to the race, while this "inward light" is given only to the favored of God.[1]

[1] Joseph John Gurney, *The Distinguishing Views and Practices*

The non-juror, William Law, emphatically says: "The Christian that rejects the necessity of immediate divine inspiration, pleads the whole cause of infidelity; he has nothing to prove the goodness of his own Christianity, but that which equally proves to the Deist the goodness of his infidelity."[1] That by prayer the path of duty will be made clear, is a universal doctrine.

The extent to which the gift of inspiration is supposed to be granted is largely a matter of church government. Where authority prevails, it is apt to be confined to those in power. Where religion is regarded as chiefly subjective and individual, it is conceded that any pious votary may become the receptacle of such special light.

Experience, however, has too often shown that inspiration teaches such contradictory doctrines that they are incompatible with any standard. The indefinite splitting of Protestant sects has convinced all clear thinkers that the claim of the early Confessions to a divinely given

---

of the Society of Friends, pp. 58, 59, 76, 78. An easy consequence of this view was to place the decrees of the internal monitor above the written word. This was advocated mainly by Elias Hicks, who expressed his doctrine in the words: "As no spring can rise higher than its fountain, so likewise the Scriptures can only direct to the fountain whence they originated—the Spirit of Truth." *Letters of Elias Hicks,* p. 228 (Phila., 1861).

[1] *Address to the Clergy,* p. 67.

power of distinguishing the true from the false has been a mistaken supposition. As a proof to an unbeliever, such a gift could avail nothing; and as evidence to one's own mind, it can only be accepted by those who deliberately shut their eyes to the innumerable contradictions it offers.[1]

While, therefore, in this, if anywhere, we perceive the only at once fit and definite answer to prayer, and find that this is acknowledged by all faiths, from the savage to the Christian, it would seem that this answer is a fallacious and futile one. The teachings of inspiration are infinitely discrepant and contradictory, and often plainly world-wide from the truth they pretend to embody. The case seems hopeless; yet, as religion of any kind without prayer is empty, there has been a proper unwillingness to adopt the conclusion just stated.

The distinction has been made that "the inspiration of the Christian is altogether *subjective*, and directed to the moral improvement of the individual,"[2] not to facts of history or questions of science, even exegetic science. The term *illumination* has been preferred for it, and while it is still defined as "a spiritual intelligence which brings truth within the range of

[1] See an intelligent note on this subject in the Rev. Wm. Lee's work, entitled *The Inspiration of the Holy Scriptures*, pp. 44, 47 (London and New York, 1857).
[2] Rev. William Lee, *u. s.*, p. 243.

mental apprehension by a kind of intuition,"[1] this truth has reference only to immediate matters of individual faith and practice. The Roman church allows more latitude than this, as it sanctions revelations concerning events, but not concerning doctrines.[2]

Looked at narrowly, the advantage which inspiration has been to religions has not so much depended on what it taught, as on its strength as a psychological motive power. As a general mental phenomenon it does not so much concern knowledge as belief; its province is to teach faith rather than facts. No conviction can equal that which arises from an assertion of God directly to ourselves. The force of the argument lies not in the question whether he did address us, but whether we believe he did. As a stimulus to action, prayer thus rises to a prime power.

Belief is considered by Professor Bain and his school to be the ultimate postulate, the final ground of intellection. It is of the utmost importance, however,—and this Professor Bain fails to do—to distinguish between two kinds of belief. There are men who believe and others who disbelieve the Koran or the Bible; I can

---

[1] Blunt, *Dictionary of Doctrinal and Historical Theology*, s. v.

[2] There is a carefully written essay on the views of the Romish Church on this subject, preceding *The Revelations of Saint Brigida* (N. Y. 1875).

accept or reject the historical existence of King Arthur or Napoleon; but, if I understand them, I cannot disbelieve the demonstrations of Euclid, nor the relations of subject and object, nor the formal laws of thought. No sane man, acquainted with the properties of numbers, can believe that twice three are ten, or that a thing can be thought as other than itself. These truths that "we cannot help believing," I have defined in the first chapter as absolute truths. They do not come to us through testimony and induction, but through a process variously called "immediate perception," "apprehension," or "intuition," a process long known but never satisfactorily explained.

All such truths are analytic, that is, they are true, not merely for a given time or place, but at all times and places conceivable, or, time and space out of the question, they still remain formally true. Of course, therefore, they cannot refer to historic occurrences nor phenomena. The modern position, that truth lies in facts, must be forsaken, and with the ancients, we must place it in ideas.

If we define inspiration as that condition of mind which is in the highest degree sensitive to the presence of such truth, we have of it the only worthy idea which it is possible to frame. The object of scientific investigation is to reach a truth which can neither be denied nor doubted. If religion is willing to content itself with any lower form of truth, it cannot support its claims to respect, let alone reverence.

It may be said that the subjects with which the religious sentiment concerns itself are not such as are capable of this absolute expression. This is, however, disclaimed by all great reformers, and by none more emphatically than by him who said: "Heaven and earth shall pass away, but my statements ($\lambda o\gamma o\iota$) shall not pass away." There is clear reference here to absolute truths. If what we know of God, duty and life, is not capable of expression except in historic narrative and synthetic terms, the sooner we drop their consideration the better. That form sufficed for a time, but can no longer, when a higher is generally known. As the mathematical surpasses the historic truth, so the former is in turn transcended by the purely logical, and in this, if anywhere, religion must rest its claims for recognition. Here is the arena of the theology of the future, not in the decrees of councils, nor in the records of past time.

Inspiration, in its religious sense, we may, therefore, define to be that condition of mind in which the truths relating to deity and duty become in whole or in part the subjects of immediate perception.

That such a condition is possible will be

granted. Every reformer who has made a permanent betterment in the religion of his time has possessed it in some degree. He who first conceived the Kosmos under logical unity as an orderly whole, had it in singular power; so too had he who looking into the mind became aware of its purposive laws which are the everlasting warrants of duty. Some nations have possessed it in remarkable fulness, none more so than the descendants of Abraham, from himself, who left his kindred and his father's house at the word of God, through many eminent seers down to Spinoza, who likewise forsook his tribe to obey the inspirations vouchsafed him; surpassing them all, Jesus of Nazareth, to whose mind, as he waxed in wisdom, the truth unfolded itself in such surpassing clearness that neither his immediate disciples nor any generations since have fathomed all the significance of his words.

Such minds do not need development and organic transmission of thought to enrich their stores. We may suppose the organization of their brains to be so perfect that their functions are always accordant with true reasoning, so self-prompting, that a hint of the problem is all they ask to arrive at its demonstration. Blaise Pascal, when a boy of twelve, whose education had been carefully restrained, once asked his father what is geometry. The latter replied that it is a method devised to draw figures correctly, but forbade any further inquiry about it. On this hint Pascal, by himself, unassisted, without so much as knowing the name of a line or circle, reached in a few weeks to the demonstration of the thirty-second problem of the first book of Euclid! Is it not possible for a mind equally productive of religious truth to surpass with no less ease its age on such subjects?

As what Newton so well called "patient thought," constant application, prolonged attention, is the means on which even great minds must rely in order to reach the sempiternal verities of science, so earnest continued prayer is that which all teachers prescribe as the only avenue to inspiration in its religious sense. While this may be conceded, collaterals of the prayer have too often been made to appear trivial and ridiculous.

In the pursuit of inspiration the methods observed present an interesting similarity. The votary who aspires to a communion with the god, shuts himself out from the distraction of social intercourse and the disturbing allurements of the senses. In the solitude of the forest or the cell, with complete bodily inaction, he gives himself to fasting and devotion, to a concentration of all his mind on the one object of his wish, the expected revelation. Waking and sleeping he banishes all other topics of thought, perhaps by an incessant repetition of a formula, until at last the moment comes, as it surely will come in some access of hallucination, furor or ecstasy, the unfailing accompaniments of excessive mental strain, when the mist seems to roll away from the mortal vision, the inimical powers which darkened the mind are baffled, and the word of the Creator makes itself articulate to the creature.

Take any connected account of the revelation of the divine will, and this history is substantially the same. It differs but little whether told of Buddha Sakyamuni, the royal seer of Kapilavastu, or by Catherine Wabose, the Chipeway squaw,[1] concerning the *Revelations* of St. Gertrude of Nivelles or of Saint Brigida, or in the homely language of the cobbler George Fox.

For six years did Sakyamuni wander in the forest, practising the mortifications of the flesh and combatting the temptations of the devil, before the final night when, after overcoming the crowning enticements of beauty, power and wealth, at a certain moment he became the " awakened," and knew himself in all his previous births, and with that knowledge soared above the "divine illusion" of existence. In the cave of Hari, Mohammed fasted and prayed until " the night of

---

[1] Chusco or Catherine Wabose, " the prophetess of Chegoimegon," has left a full and psychologically most valuable account of her inspiration. It is published in Schoolcraft's *History and Statistics of the Indian Tribes*, Vol. I., p. 390, sqq.

the divine decisions ;" then he saw the angel Gabriel approach and inspire him :

> "A revelation was revealed to him :
> One terrible in power taught it him,
> Endowed with wisdom. With firm step stood he,
> There, where the horizon is highest,
> Then came he near and nearer,
> A matter of two bowshots or closer,
> And he revealed to his servant a revelation;
> He has falsified not what he saw."[1]

With not dissimilar preparation did George Fox seek the "openings" which revealed to him the hollowness of the Christianity of his day, in contrast to the truth he found. In his *Journal* he records that for months he "fasted much, walked around in solitary places, and sate in hollow trees and lonesome places, and frequently in the night walked mournfully about." When the word of truth came to him it was of a sudden, "through the immediate opening of the invisible spirit." Then a new life commenced for him: "Now was I come up in Spirit through the flaming sword into the Paradise of God. All things were new; all the creation gave another smell unto me than before." The healing virtues of all herbs were straightway made known to him, and the needful truths about the kingdom of God.[2]

---

[1] *The Koran*, Sura liii. This is in date one of the earliest suras.
[2] *The Journal of George Fox*, pp. 59, 67, 69.

These are portraitures of the condition of *entheasm*. Its lineaments are the same, find it where we may.

How is this similarity to be explained? Is it that this alleged inspiration is always but the dream of a half-crazed brain? The deep and real truths it has now and then revealed, the noble results it has occasionally achieved, do not allow this view. A more worthy explanation is at hand.

These preliminaries of inspiration are in fact but a parody, sometimes a caricature, of the most intense intellectual action as shown in the efforts of creative thought. The physiological characteristics of such mental episodes indicate a lowering of the animal life, the respiration is faint and slow, the pulse loses in force and frequency, the nerves of special sense are almost inhibited, the eye is fixed and records no impression, the ear registers no sound, necessary motions are performed unconsciously, the condition approaches that of trance. There is also an alarming similarity at times between the action of genius and of madness, as is well known to alienists.

When the creative thought appears, it does so suddenly; it breaks upon the mind when partly engaged with something else as an instantaneous flash, apparently out of connection with previous efforts. This is the history of all great discoveries, and it has been abundantly illustrated from the lives of inventors, artists, poets and mathematicians. The links of such a mental procedure we do not know. "The product of inspiration, genius, is incomprehensible to itself. Its activity proceeds on no beaten track, and we seek in vain to trace its footsteps. There is no warrant for the value of its efforts. This it can alone secure through voluntary submission to law. All its powers are centred in the energy of production, and none is left for idle watching of the process." [1]

The prevalent theory of the day is that this mental action is one essentially hidden from the mind itself. The name "unconscious cerebration" has been proposed for it by Dr. Carpenter, and he has amply and ably illustrated its peculiarities. But his theory has encountered just criticism, and I am persuaded does not meet the requirements of the case. Whether at such moments the mind actually receives some impulse from without, as is the religious theory, or, as science more willingly teaches, certain associations are more easily achieved when the mind is partially engaged with other trains of ideas, we cannot be sure. We can only say of it, in the words of Dr. Henry Maudsley, the result "is truly an inspiration, coming we know not whence." Whatever it is, we recognize in

[1] Wilhelm von Humboldt, *Gesammelte Werke*, Bd. iv., s. 278.

it the original of that of which religious hallucination is the counterfeit presentment. So similar are the processes that their liability to be confounded has been expressly guarded against.[1]

The prevalence of such caricatures does not prove the absence of the sterling article. They rather show that the mind is conscious of the possibility of reaching a frame or mood in which it perceives what it seeks, immediately and correctly. Buddhism distinctly asserts this to be the condition of " the stage of intuitive insight ; " and Protestant Christianity commenced with the same opinion. Every prayer for guidance in the path of duty assumes it. The error is in applying such a method where it is incompatible, to facts of history and the phenomena of physical force. Confined to the realm of ideas, to which alone the norm of the true and untrue is applicable, there is no valid evidence against, and many theoretical reasons for, respecting prayer as a fit psychological preparation for those obscure and unconscious processes, through which the mind accomplishes its best work.

The intellect, exalted by dwelling upon the sublimest subjects of thought, warmed into

[1] In his treatise *De Veritate*, itself the subject, as its author thought, of a special revelation, Lord Herbert of Cherbury, gives as one of the earmarks of a real revelation : "ut afflatum Divini numinis sentias, ita enim internæ Facultatum circa veritatem operationes a revelationibus externis distinguuntur." p. 226.

highest activity by the flames of devotion, spurning as sterile and vain the offers of time and the enticements of sense, may certainly be then in the mood fittest to achieve its greatest victories. But no narrowed heaven must cloud it, no man-made god obstruct its gaze. Free from superstition and prejudice, it must be ready to follow wherever the voice of reason shall lead it. All inspired men have commenced by freeing themselves from inherited forms of belief in order that with undiverted attention they might listen to the promptings of the divinity within their souls. One of the greatest of them and one the most free from the charge of prejudice, has said that to this end prayer is the means.[1]

He who believes that the ultimate truth is commensurate with reason, finds no stumbling-block in the doctrine that there may be laws through whose action inspiration is the enlightenment of mind as it exists in man, by mind as it underlies the motions which make up matter. The truth thus reached is not the formulæ of the Calculus, nor the verbiage of the Dialectic, still less the events of history, but that which gives what validity they have to all of these, and moreover imparts to the will and the conscience their power to govern conduct.

[1] Spinoza, *Espistolæ et Responsionnes*, Ep. xxxiv.

THE MYTH AND THE MYTHICAL CYCLES.

SUMMARY.

Myths are inspirations concerning the Unknown. Science treats them as apperceptions of the relations of man and nature. Moments of their growth, as treated by mythological science. Their similar forms, explained variously, the topic of the philosophy of mythology. The ante-mythical period. Myths have centred chiefly around three subjects, each giving rise to a Mythical Cycle.

I. The Epochs of Nature.

The idea of Time led to the myth of a creation. This starting the question, What was going on before creation? recourse was had to the myth of recurrent epochs. The last epoch gave origin to the Flood Myths; the coming one to that of the Day of Judgment.

II. The Paradise lost and to be re-gained.

To man, the past and the future are ever better than the present. He imagines a Golden Age in the past and believes it will return. The material Paradise he dreams of in his ruder conditions, becomes a spiritual one with intellectual advancement. The basis of this belief.

III. The Hierarchy of the Gods.

The earliest hierarchy is a dual classification of the gods into those who help and those who hinder the fruition of desire. Light and darkness typify the contrast. Divinity thus conceived under numerical separateness. Monotheisms do not escape this. The triune nature of single gods. The truly religious and only philosophic notion of divinity is under logical, not mathematical unity. This discards mythical conceptions.

CHAPTER V.

THE MYTH AND THE MYTHICAL CYCLES.

RETURNING again to the definition of the elemental religious sentiment—" a Wish whose fruition depends upon unknown power " — it enables us to class all those notions, opinions and narratives, which constitute mythologies, creeds and dogmas, as theories respecting the nature and action of the unknown power. Of course they are not recognized as theories. They arise unconsciously or are received by tradition, oral or written, and always come with the stamp of divinity through inspiration and revelation. None but a god can tell the secrets of the gods.

Therefore they are the most sacred of all things, and they partake of the holiness and immutability which belong to the unknown power itself. To misplace a vowel point in copying the sacred books was esteemed a sin by the Rabbis, and a pious Mussulman will not employ the same pen to copy a verse of the Koran and an ordinary letter. There are many Christians who suppose the saying : " Heaven and earth shall pass away, but My Words shall not pass away," has reference to the words of the Old and New Testament. "What shall remain to us," asked Ananda, the disciple of Buddha, "when thou shalt have gone hence into Nirvana?" "My Word (*dharma*)," replied the Master. Names thus came to be as holy as the objects to which they referred. So sacred was that of Jehovah to the Israelites that its original sound was finally lost. Such views are consistent enough to the Buddhist, who, assuming all existence to be but imaginary, justly infers that the name is full as much as the object.

The science of mythology has made long strides in the last half century. It has left far behind it the old euhemeristic view that the myth is a distorted historical tradition, as well as the theories not long since in vogue, that it was a system of natural philosophy, a device of shrewd rulers, or as Bacon thought, a series of "instructive fables." The primitive form of the myth is now recognized to be made up from the notions which man gains of the manifestations of force in external nature, in their supposed relations to himself. In technical language it may be defined as *the apperception of man and nature under synthetic conceptions.*[1]

[1] In this definition the word *apperception* is used in the sense assigned it by Professor Lazarus—the perception modified by imagination and memory. "Mythologie ist eine Apperceptionsform der Natur und des Menschen." (*Zeitschrift für Völ-*

This primitive form undergoes numerous changes, to trace and illustrate which, has been the special task assumed by the many recent writers on mythology. In some instances these changes are owing to the blending of the myth with traditions of facts, forming a quasi-historical narrative, the *saga ;* in others, elaborated by a poetic fancy and enriched by the imagination, it becomes a fairy tale, the *märchen.* Again, the myth being a product of creative thought, existing in words only, as language changes, it alters through forgetfulness of the earlier meanings of words, through similarities in sounds deceiving the ear, or through a confusion of the literal with the metaphorical signification of the same word. The character of languages also favors or retards such changes, pliable and easily modified ones, such as those of the American Indians, and in a less degree those of the Aryan nations, favoring a developed mythology, while rigid and monosyllabic ones, as the Chinese and Semitic types, offer fewer facilities to such variations. Furthermore, tribal or national history, the peculiar dif-

kerpsychologie, Bd. i., s. 44). Most recent mythologists omit the latter branch of the definition ; for instance. " A myth is in its origin an explanation by the uncivilized mind of some natural phenomenon." (John Fiske. *Myths and Myth Makers,* p. 21). This is to omit that which gives the myth its only claim to be a product of the religious sentiment. Schopenhauer, in calling dogmas and myths " the metaphysics of the people," fell into the same error. Religion, as such, is always concrete.

ficulties which retard the growth of a community, and the geographical and climatic character of its surroundings, give prominence to certain features in its mythology, and to the absence of others. Myths originally diverse are blended, either unconsciously, as that of the Roman Saturn with the Greek Cronus; or consciously, as when the medieval missionaries transferred the deeds of the German gods to Christian saints. Lastly, the prevailing temperament of a nation, its psychology, gives a strong color to its mythical conceptions, and imprints upon them the national peculiarities.

The judicious student of mythology must carefully weigh all these formative agents, and assign each its value. They are all present in every mythology, but in varying force. His object is accomplished when he can point out the causal relation between the various features of a myth and these governing agencies.

Such is the science of mythology. The philosophy of mythology undertakes to set forth the unities of form which exist in various myths, and putting aside whatever of this uniformity is explainable historically, proposes to illustrate from what remains the intellectual need myths were unconsciously framed to gratify, to measure their success in this attempt, and if they have not been wholly successful, to point out why and in what respect they have failed. In a study preliminary to the present one, I have attempted to apply the rules of mythological science to the limited area of the native American race; in the present chapter I shall deal mainly with the philosophy of mythology.

The objection may be urged at starting that there is no such unity of form in myths as the philosophy of mythology assumes; that if it appears, it is always explainable historically.

A little investigation sets this objection aside. Certain features must be common to all myths. A divinity must appear in them and his doings with men must be recorded. A reasonable being can hardly think at all without asking himself, "Whence come I, my fellows, and these things which I see? And what will become of us all?" So some myth is sure to be created at an early stage of thought which the parent can tell the child, the wise man his disciple, containing responses to such questions.

But this reasoning from probability is needless, for the similarity of mythical tales in very distant nations, where no hypothesis of ancient intercourse is justified, is one of the best ascertained and most striking discoveries of modern mythological investigation.[1] The general char-

[1] Half a century ago the learned Mr. Faber, in his *Origin of Pagan Idolatry*, expressed his astonishment at "the singular, minute and regular accordance" between the classical myths. That accordance has now been discovered to be world-wide.

acter of "solar myths" is familiar to most readers, and the persistency with which they have been applied to the explanation of generally received historical facts, as well as to the familiar fairy tales of childhood, has been pushed so far as to become the subject of satire and caricature. The myths of the Dawn have been so frequently brought to public notice in the popular writings of Professor Max Müller, that their general distribution may be taken as well known. The same may be said of the storm myths. Wilhelm von Humboldt, who thought deeply on the religious nature of man, said early in this century: "Wholly similar myths can very readily arise in different localities, each independent of the others."[1]

This similarity is in a measure owing to the similar impressions which the same phenomenon, the sunrise or the thunder-storm for instance, makes on the mind—and to this extent the science of mythology is adequate to its explanation. But that it falls short is so generally acknowledged, that various other explanations have been offered.

These may be classed as the skeptical explanation, which claims that the likeness of the myths is vastly exaggerated and much more the work of the scholar at his desk than of the

[1] "Ganz gleiche Mythen können sehr füglich, jede selbstständig, an verschiedenen Oerter emporkommen."*Briefe an Woelcker.*

honest worshipper; the historical explanation, which suggests unrecorded proselytisms, forgotten communications and the possible original unity of widely separated nations; the theological explanations, often discrepant, one suggesting caricatures of the sacred narrative inspired by the Devil, another reminiscences of a primeval inspiration, and a third the unconscious testimony of heathendom to orthodoxy;[1] and lastly the metaphysical explanation, which seems at present to be the fashionable one, expressed nearly alike by Steinthal and Max Müller, which cuts the knot by crediting man with "an innate consciousness of the Absolute," or as Renan puts it, "a profound instinct of deity."

The philosophy of mythology, differing from all these, finding beyond question similarities which history cannot unriddle, interprets them by no incomprehensible assumption, but by the identity of the laws of thought acting on similar impressions under the guidance of known categories of thought. Nor does it stop here, but proceeds to appraise these results by the general scheme of truth and error. It asks for what

[1] The last two are the modern orthodox theories, supported by Bryant, Faber, Trench, De Maistre and Sepp. Medieval Christianity preferred the direct agency of the Devil. Primitive Christianity leaned to the opinion that the Grecian and Roman myth makers had stolen from the sacred writings of the Jews.

psychological purpose man has so universally imagined for himself gods—pure creations of his fancy;—whether that purpose can now or will ultimately be better attained by an exercise of his intellect more in accordance with the laws of right reasoning; and thus seeking to define the genuine food of the religious desire, estimates the quality and value of each mythological system by the nearness of its approach to this standard.

The philosophy of mythology, starting with the wish or prayer as the unit of religious thought, regards all myths as theories about the unknown power which is supposed to grant or withhold the accomplishment of the wish. These theories are all based upon the postulate of the religious sentiment, that there is order in things; but they differ from scientific theories in recognizing volition as an efficient cause of order.

The very earliest efforts at religious thought do not rise to the formation of myths, that is, connected narratives about supernatural beings. All unknown power is embraced under a word which does not convey the notion of personality; single exhibitions of power which threaten man's life are supposed to be the doings of an unseen person, often of a deceased man, whose memory survives; but any general theory of a hierarchy, or of the world or man, is not yet visible. Even such immature notions are, however, so far as they go, framed within the category of causality; only, the will of the god takes the place of all other force. This stage of religious thought has been called Animism, a name which does not express its peculiarity, which is, that all force is not only supposed to proceed from mind, but through what metaphysicians call "immanent volition," that is, through will independent of relation. Mind as "emanant volition," in unison with matter and law, the "seat of law," to use an expression of Professor Boole's, may prove the highest conception of force.

As the slowly growing reason reached more general notions, the law which prescribes unity as a condition of thought led man early in his history to look upon nature as one, and to seek for some one law of its changes; the experience of social order impressed him with the belief that the unseen agencies around him also bore relations to each other, and acknowledged subjection to a leader; and the pangs of sickness, hunger and terror to which he was daily exposed, and more than all the "last and greatest of all terribles, death," which he so often witnessed, turned his early meditations toward his own origin and destiny.

Around these three subjects of thought his fancy busied itself, striving to fabricate some theory which would solve the enigmas which his reason everywhere met, some belief which would relieve him from the haunting horror of the unknown. Hence arose three great cycles of myths, which recur with strangely similar physiognomies in all continents and among all races. They are the myths of the Epochs of Nature, the Hierarchy of the Gods, and of the Paradise lost but to be regained. Wherever we turn, whether to the Assyrian tablets or to the verses of the Voluspa, to the crude fancies of the red man of the new world or the black man of the African plateau, to the sacred books of the modern Christian or of the ancient Brahman, we find these same questions occupying his mind, and in meaning and in form the same solutions proffered. Through what intellectual operations he reached these solutions, and their validity, as tested by the known criteria of truth, it is the province of the philosophy of mythology to determine.

Let us study the psychological growth of the myth of the Epochs of Nature. This tells of the World, its beginning, its convulsions and its ending, and thus embraces the three minor cycles of the cosmogonical, the cataclysmal and the eschatological myths.

Nature is known to man only as *force*, which manifests itself in *change*. He is so constituted that " the idea of an event, a change, without the idea of a cause, is impossible " to him. But in passing from the occurrence to its cause the idea of Time is unavoidable; it presents itself as the one inevitable condition of change; itself unwearing, it wears out all else; it includes all existence, as the greater does the less; and as "causation is necessarily within existence,"[1] time is beyond existence and includes the non-existent as well. Whatever it creates, it also destroys; and as even the gods are but existences, it will swallow them. It renders vain all pleasures, and carries the balm of a certain oblivion for all woes.

This oppressive sense of time, regarded not in its real meaning as one of the conditions of perception, but as an active force destroying thought as well as motion, recurs continually in mythology. To the Greek, indefinite time as Cronos, was the oldest of the gods, begetting numberless children, but with unnatural act consuming them again; while definite time, as the Horæ, were the blithe goddesses of the order in nature and the recurrent seasons. Osiris, supreme god of the Egyptians, was born of a yet older god, Sev, Time. Adonis and Aeon acknowledge the same parentage.[2] The ancient Arab spoke of time (*dahr, zaman*) as the final, defining principle; as uniting and separating all things; and as swallowing one thing after another as the camel drains the water from a

---

[1] Sir Wm. Hamilton, *Lectures on Metaphysics*. Appendix, p. 691.

[2] Creuzer, *Symbolik und Mythologie*, Bd. ii., s. 107.

trough.¹ In the Koran it is written: "Time alone destroys us." Here and there, through the sacred songs of the Parsees, composed long before Aristotle wrote, beyond all the dust and noise of the everlasting conflict of good and evil, of Ahura Mazda and Anya-Mainyus, there are glimpses of a deeper power, Zeruana Akerana, Eternal Duration, unmoved by act or thought, in the face of which these bitter opponents are seen to be children, brethren, "twin sons of Time."² The Alexandrian Gnostics, in their explanations of Christian dogmas, identify Aeon, infinite time, with God the Father, as the source and fount of existence; not merely as a predicate of the highest, but the Highest himself.

This heavy-weighing sense of the infinity of duration, and the urgency of escaping from the weariness of thinking it, led to the construction of the myth of the Creation. Man devised it so that he might be able to say, " in the beginning." But a new difficulty met him at the threshold—as change must be in existence, "we cannot think of a change from non-existence to existence." His only refuge was to select some apparently primordial, simple, homogeneous substance from which, by the exertion of volition,

---

¹ Th. Nöldeke, *Zeitschrift für Völkerpsychologie*, Bd. iii., s. 131.

² See a note of Prof. Spiegel to Yaçna, 29, of the *Khordah-Avesta*.

things came into being. The one which most naturally suggested itself was *water*.[1] This does in fact cover and hide the land, and the act of creation was often described as the emerging of the dry land from the water; it dissolves and wears away the hard rock; and, diminishing all things, itself neither diminishes nor increases. Therefore nearly all cosmogonical myths are but variations of that one familiar to us all : " And God said, Let the waters under the heaven be gathered together in one place, and let the dry land appear; and it was so." The manifestation of the primordial energy was supposed to have been akin to that which is shown in organic reproduction. The myths of the primeval egg from which life proceeded, of the mighty bird typical of the Holy Spirit which " brooded " upon the waters, of Love developing the Kosmos from the Chaos, of the bull bringing the world from the waters, of Protogonus, the "eggborn," the "multispermed," and countless others, point to the application of one or the other, or of both these explanations.[2]

In them the early thinkers found some rest:

[1] Ἡ ὑγρα φυσις αρχη και γενεσις παντων.
Plutarch, *De Iside*.
According to the Koran and the Jewish Rabbis, the throne of God rested on the primeval waters from which the earth was produced. See a note in Rodwell's translation of the Koran, *Sura*. xi.

[2] I have discussed some of these myths in the seventh chapter of the *Myths of the New World*.

but not for long. The perplexity of the presence of this immediate order of things seemed solved; but another kept obtruding itself: what was going on before that " beginning ? " Vain to stifle the inquiry by replying, " nothing."[1] For time, which knows no beginning, was there, still building, still destroying; nothing can be put to it, nor anything taken from it. What then is left but the conclusion of the Preacher : " That which hath been, is now; and that which is to be, hath already been ? " Regarding time as a form of force, the only possible history of the material universe is that it is a series of destructions and restorations, force latent evolving into force active or energy, and this dissipated and absorbed again into latency.

Expressed in myths, these destructions and restorations are the Epochs of Nature. They are an essential part of the religious traditions of the Brahmans, Persians, Parsees, Greeks, Egyptians, Jews, Mexicans, Mayas, and of all nations who have reached a certain stage of culture. The length of the intervening periods may widely differ. The kalpa or great year of the Brahmans is so long that were a cube of

[1] How it troubled the early Christians who dared not adopt the refuge of the Epochs of Nature, may be seen in the *Confessions* of St. Augustine, Lib. XI, cap. 10, et seq. He quotes the reply of one pushed by the inquiry, what God was doing before creation : "He was making a hell for inquisitive busy-bodies." *Alta spectantibus gehennas parabat.*

granite a hundred yards each way brushed once in a century by a soft cloth, it would be quite worn to dust before the kalpa would close: or, as some Christians believe, there may be but six thousand years, six days of God in whose sight "a thousand years are as one day," between the creation and the cremation of the world, from when it rose from the waters until it shall be consumed by the fire.

There were also various views about the agents and the completeness of these periodical destructions. In the Norse mythology and in the doctrine of Buddhism, not one of the gods can survive the fire of the last day. Among the Greeks, great Jove alone will await the appearance of the virgin world after the icy winter and the fiery summer of the Great Year. The Brahmans hold that the higher classes of gods outlive the wreck of things which, at the close of the day of Brahm, involves all men and many divinities in elemental chaos; while elsewhere, in the later Puranas and in the myths of Mexico, Peru, and Assyria, one or a few of the race of man escape a deluge which is universal, and serve to people the new-made earth. This latter supposition, in its application to the last epoch of nature, is the origin of the myth of the Flood.

In its general features and even in many details, the story of a vast overflow which drowned the world, and from which by the timely succor of divinity some man was preserved, and after the waters had subsided became the progenitor of the race, is exceedingly common among distant tribes, where it is impossible to explain it as a reminiscence of a historic occurrence, or by community of religious doctrine. In Judea Noah, in India Manu, in Chaldea Xisuthrus, in Assyria Oannes, in Aztlan Nata, in Algonkin tradition Messou, in Brazil Monan, etc., are all heroes of similar alleged occurrences. In all of them the story is but a modification of that of the creation in time from the primeval waters.[1]

"As it was once, so it shall be again," and as the present age of the world wears out, the myth

---

[1] Many interesting references to the Oriental flood-myth may be found in Cory's *Ancient Fragments*. See also, Dr. Fr. Windischmann, *Die Ursagen der Arischen Völker*, pp. 4–10. It is probable that in very ancient Semitic tradition Adam was represented as the survivor of a flood anterior to that of Noah. Maimonides relates that the Sabians believed the world to be eternal, and called Adam "the Prophet of the Moon," which symbolized, as we know from other sources, the deity of water. Rabbi Moses Ben Maimon, *More Nevochim*, cap. iv. In early Christian symbolism Christ was called "the true Noah"; the dove accompanied him also, and as through Noah came "salvation by wood and water," so through Christ came "salvation by spirit and water." (See St. Cyril of Jerusalem's *Catechetical Lectures*, Lect. xvii., cap. 10). The fish ($\imath \chi \theta \nu \varsigma$) was the symbol of Christ as well as of Oannes. As the second coming of Christ was to be the destruction of the world, how plainly appear the germs of the myth of the Epochs of Nature in the Judæo-Christian mind!

teaches that things will once more fall back to universal chaos. "The expectation of the end of the world is a natural complement to the belief in its periodical destructions." It is taught with distinctness by all religious systems, by the prophetess in the Voluspa, by the Hebrew seers,[1] by the writer of the Apocalypse, by the Eastern sages, Persian and Indian, by the Roman Sibyl, and among the savage and semi-civilized races of the New World.

Often that looked for destruction was associated with the divine plans for man. This was an addition to the simplicity of the original myth, but an easy and a popular one. The Indian of our prairies still looks forward to the time when the rivers shall rise, and submerging the land sweep from its surface the pale-faced intruders, and restore it to its original owners. Impatient under the ceaseless disappointments of life, and worn out with the pains which seem inseparable from this condition of things, the believer gives up his hopes for this world, and losing his faith in the final conquest of the good, thinks it only attainable by the total annihilation of the present conditions. He looks for it, therefore, in the next great age, in the new

[1] Besides the expressions in the Book of Ecclesiastes and the later prophets, the doctrine is distinctly announced in one of the most sublime of the Psalms (xc), one attributed to "Moses the Man of God."

heaven and the new earth, when the spirit of evil shall be bound and shut up, and the chosen people possess the land, "and grow up as calves of the stall."[1]

This is to be inaugurated by the Day of Judgment, "the day of wrath, the dreadful day," in which God is to come in his power and pronounce his final decrees on those who have neglected the observance due him. The myth, originally one relating to the procession of natural forces, thus assumed with the increasing depth of the religious sentiment more and more a moral and subjective coloring, until finally its old and simple form was altogether discarded, or treated as symbolic only.

The myth of the Epochs of Nature was at first a theory to account for the existing order of nature. For a long time it satisfied the inquiring mind, if not with a solution at least with an answer to its queries. After geologic science had learned to decipher the facts of the world's growth as written on the stones which orb it, the religious mind fondly identified the upheavals and cataclysms there recorded with those which its own fancy had long since fabricated. The stars and suns, which the old seer thought would fall from heaven in the day of wrath, were seen to be involved in motions far beyond the pale of

[1] Malachi, ch. iv., v. 2.

man's welfare, and, therefore, the millennial change was confined to the limits of our planet. Losing more and more of its original form as an attempted explanation of natural phenomena, the myth now exists in civilized nations as an allegorical type of man's own history and destiny, and thus is slowly merging into an episode of the second great cycle of the mythus, that of the Paradise lost and regained. It, too, finds its interpretation in psychology.

Broadly surveying the life of man, philosophers have found in it much matter fit either for mockery or tears. We are born with a thirst for pleasure; we learn that pain alone is felt. We ask health; and having it, never notice it till it is gone. In the ardent pursuit of enjoyment, we waste our capacity of appreciation. Every sweet we gain is sauced with a bitter. Our eyes forever bent on the future, which can never be ours, we fritter away the present, which alone we possess. Ere we have got ourselves ready to live, we must die. Fooling ourselves even here, we represent death as the portal to joy unspeakable; and forthwith discredit our words by avoiding it in every possible way.

Pitiable spectacle of weakness and folly, is it capable of any explanation which can redeem man from the imputation of unreason? Is Wisdom even here justified of her children by some deeper law of being?

The theologian explains it as the unrest of the soul penned in its house of clay; the physiologist attributes it to the unceasing effort of organic functions to adapt themselves to ever varying external conditions. They are both right, for the theologian, were his words translated into the language of science, refers to the *effort to adapt condition to function*, which is the peculiar faculty of intelligence, and which alone renders man unable to accept the comfort of merely animal existence, an inability which he need never expect to outlive, for it will increase in exact proportion to his mental development. Action, not rest, as I have elsewhere said, must be his ideal of life.

In even his lowest levels man experiences this dissatisfaction. It may there be confined to a pain he would be free from, or a pleasure he dreams of. Always the future charms him, and as advancing years increase the number of his disappointments and bring with them the pains of decrepitude, he also recurs to the past, when youth was his, and the world was bright and gay. Thus it comes that most nations speak of some earlier period of their history as one characterized by purer public virtues than the present, one when the fires of patriotism burned brighter and social harmony was more conspicuous. In rude stages of society this fancy receives real credit and ranks as a veritable record of the past, forming a Golden Age or Saturnian Era. Turned in the kaleidoscope of the mythus, it assumes yet more gorgeous hues, and becomes a state of pure felicity, an Eden or a Paradise, wherein man dwelt in joy, and from which he wandered or was driven in the old days.

It is almost needless to quote examples to show the wide distribution of this myth. The first pages of the Vendidad describe the reign of Yima in "the garden of delight," where "there was no cold wind nor violent heat, no disease and no death." The northern Buddhist tells of "the land of joy," Sukhavati, in the far west, where ruled Amitabha, "infinite Light."[1] The Edda wistfully recalls the pleasant days of good King Gudmund who once held sway in Odainsakr, where death came not.[2] Persian story has glad reminiscences of the seven hundred years that Jemschid sat on the throne of Iran, when peace and plenty were in the land.

The garden "eastward in Eden" of the Pentateuch, the land of Tulan or Tlapallan in Aztec myth, the islands of the Hesperides, the rose garden of Feridun, and a score of other legends attest with what strong yearning man seeks in

[1] C. F. Koppen, *Die Lamaische Hierarchie*, s. 28.

[2] Odainsakr, ô privative, *dain* death, *akr* land, "the land of immortal life." Saxo Grammaticus speaks of it also. Another such land faintly referred to in the Edda is Breidablick, governed by Baldur, the Light-god.

the past the picture of that perfect felicity which the present never yields.

Nor can he be persuaded that the golden age has gone, no more to return. In all conditions of progress, and especially where the load of the present was the most wearying, has he counted on a restoration to that past felicity. The paradise lost is to be regained. How it is to be done the sages are not agreed. But they of old were unanimous that some divinity must lend his aid, that some god-sent guide is needed to rescue man from the slough of wretchedness in which he hopelessly struggles.

Therefore in the new world the red men looked for the ruler who had governed their happy forefathers in the golden age, and who had not died but withdrawn mysteriously from view, to return to them, protect them, and insure them long bliss and ease. The ancient Persians expected as much from the coming of Craoshanç; the Thibetan Buddhists look to the advent of a Buddha 5000 years after Sakyamuni, one whose fortunate names are Maîtrêya, the Loving one, and Adjita, the Unconquerable;[1] and even the practical Roman, as we learn from Virgil, was not a stranger to this dream. Very many nations felt it quite as strongly as the Israelites, who from early time awaited a mighty king, the Messiah, the Anointed, of whom the Targums say: "In his

[1] C. F. Koppen, *Die Lamaische Hierarchie und Kirche*, p. 17.

days shall peace be multiplied;" "He shall execute the judgment of truth and justice on the earth;" "He shall rule over all kingdoms."

The early forms of this conception, such as here referred to, looked forward to an earthly kingdom, identified with that of the past when this was vigorous in the national mythology. Material success and the utmost physical comfort were to characterize it. It was usually to be a national apotheosis, and was not generally supposed to include the human race, though traces of this wider view might easily be quoted from Avestan, Roman, and Israelitic sources. Those who were to enjoy it were not the dead, but those who shall be living.

As the myth grew, it coalesced with that of the Epochs of Nature, and assumed grander proportions. The deliverer was to come at the close of this epoch, at the end of the world; he was to embrace the whole human kind in his kingdom; even those who died before his coming, if they had obeyed his mandates, should rise to join the happy throng; instead of a mere earthly king, he should be a supernatural visitant, even God himself; and instead of temporal pleasures only, others of a spiritual character were to be conferred. There are reasons to believe that even in this developed form the myth was familiar to the most enlightened worshippers of ancient Egypt; but it was not till some time after the doctrines of christianity had been cast into mythical moulds by the oriental fancy, that it was introduced in its completed form to modern thought. Although expressly repudiated by Jesus of Nazareth himself, and applied in maxim and parable as a universal symbol of intelligence to the religious growth of the individual and race, his followers reverted to the coarser and literal meaning, and ever since teach to a greater or less extent the chiliastic or millennial dogma, often mathematically computing, in direct defiance of his words, the exact date that event is to be expected.

If we ask the psychological construction of this myth, and the ever present conditions of man's life which have rendered him always ready to create it and loath to renounce it, we trace the former distinctly to his sense of the purposive nature of the laws of thought, and the latter to the wide difference between desire and fulfilment. His intellectual nature is framed to accord with laws which are ever present but are not authoritative; they admonish but they do not coerce; *that* is done surely though oft remotely by the consequences of their violation. At first, unaware of the true character of these laws, he fancies that if he were altogether comfortable physically, his every wish would be gratified. Slowly it dawns upon him that no material gratification can supply an intellectual craving; that this is the real want which haunts him ; and that its only satisfaction is *to think rightly*, to learn the truth. Then he sees that the millennial kingdom is " not of this world ; " that heaven and earth may pass away, but that such truth as he seeks cannot pass away; and that his first and only care should be as a faithful and wise servant to learn and revere it.

The sentiments which created this mythical cycle, based as they are now seen to be on ultimate psychological laws, are as active to-day as ever. This century has witnessed the rise of a school of powerful thinkers and true philanthropists who maintained that the noblest object is the securing to our fellow-men the greatest material comfort possible ; that the religious aspirations will do well to content themselves with this gospel of humanity ; and that the approach of the material millennium, the perfectibility of the human race, the complete adaptation of function to condition, the " distant but not uncertain final victory of Good,"[1] is susceptible of demonstration. At present, these views are undergoing modification. It is perceived with more or less distinctness that complete physical comfort is not enough to make a man happy ; that in proportion as this comfort is attained new wants develope themselves, quite as importunate, which ask what material com-

[1] John Stuart Mill, *Theism*, p. 256.

fort cannot give, and whose demand is neither for utility nor pleasurable sensation. Such wants are created by the sense of duty and the love of truth.

The main difference between the latest exponents of the utilitarian doctrines and the heralds of distinctively religious thought, is that the former consider that it is most important in the present condition of man for him to look after his material welfare; while the latter teach that if he first subject thought and life to truth and duty,"all these things will be added unto him." Wordsworth has cast this latter opinion, and the myths which are its types, into eloquent verse :

> " Paradise and groves
> Elysian, Fortunate Fields—like those of old
> Sought in the Atlantic main, why should they be
> A history only of departed things,
> Or a mere fiction of what never was ?
> For the discerning intellect of man,
> When wedded to this goodly universe
> In love and holy passion, shall find these
> A simple produce of the common day."

The incredulity and even derision with which the latter doctrine is received by " practical men," should not affright the collected thinker, as it certainly is not so chimerical as they pretend. The writer De Senancourt, not at all of a religious turn, in speculating on the shortest possible road to general happiness, concluded that if we were able to foretell the weather a reasonable time ahead, and if men would make it a rule to speak the truth as near as they can, these two conditions would remove nine-tenths of the misery in the world. The more carefully I meditate on this speculation, the better grounded it seems. The weather we are learning to know much more about than when the solitary Obermann penned his despondent dreams; but who shall predict the time when men will tell the truth?

I now pass to the third great mythical cyclus, which I have called that of the Hierarchy of the Gods. This was created in order to define that unknown power which was supposed to give to the wish frustration or fruition. It includes every statement in reference to the number, nature, history and character of supernatural beings.

The precise form under which the intellect, when the religious conception of unknown power first dawns upon it, imagines this unknown, is uncertain. Some have maintained that the earliest religions are animal worships, others that the spirits of ancestors or chiefs are the primitive gods. Local divinities and personal spirits are found in the rudest culture, while simple fetichism, or the vague shapes presented by dreams, play a large part in the most inchoate systems. The prominence of one or the other of these elements depends upon local and national momenta, which are a proper study for the science of mythology, but need not detain us here. The underlying principle in all these conceptions of divinity is that of the *res per accidens*, an accidental relation of the thought to the symbol, not a general or necessary one. This is seen in the nature of these primitive gods. They have no decided character as propitious or the reverse other than the objects they typify, but are supposed to send bad or good fortune as they happen to be pleased or displeased with the votary. No classification as good and evil deities is as yet perceptible.

This undeveloped stage of religious thought faded away, as general conceptions of man and his surroundings arose. Starting always from his wish dependent on unknown control, man found certain phenomena usually soothed his fears and favored his wishes, while others interfered with their attainment and excited his alarm. This distinction, directly founded on his sensations of pleasure and pain, led to a general, more or less rigid, classification of the unknown, into two opposing classes of beings, the one kindly disposed, beneficent, good, the other untoward, maleficent, evil.

At first this distinction had in it nothing of a *moral* character. It is in fact a long time before this is visible, and to-day but two or three religions acknowledge it even theoretically. All, however, which claim historical position set up a dual hierarchy in the divine realms. Ahuramazda and Anya-mainyus, God and Satan, Jove and Pluto, Pachacamac and Supay, Enigorio and

Enigohatgea are examples out of hundreds that might be adduced.

The fundamental contrast of pleasure and pain might be considered enough to explain this duality. But in fact it is even farther reaching. The emotions are dual as well as the sensations, as we have seen in the first chapter. All the operations of the intellect are dichotomic, and in mathematical logic must be expressed by an equation of the second degree. Subject and object must be understood as polar pairs, and in physical science polarization, contrast of properties corresponding to contrast of position, is a universal phenomenon. Analogy, therefore, vindicates the assumption that the unknown, like the known, is the field of the operation of contradictory powers.

A variety of expression is given this philosophic notion in myths. In Egypt, Syria, Greece and India the contrast was that of the sexes, the male and female principles as displayed in the operations of nature. The type of all is that very ancient Phrygian cult in which by the side of Ma, mother of mountains and mistress of herds, stood Papas, father of the race of shepherds and inventor of the rustic pipe.[1] Quite characteristic was the classification of the gods worshipped by the miners and metal workers of Phrygian Ida. This was into right and left,

Creuzer, *Symbolik und Mythologie*, Bd. II., s. 47

and the general name of Dactyli, Fingers, was given them. The right gods broke the spells which the left wove, the right pointed out the ore which the left had buried, the right disclosed the remedies for the sickness which the left had sent. This venerable division is still retained when we speak of a *sinister* portent, or a *right* judgment. It is of physiological interest as showing that " dextral pre-eminence " or right-handedness was prevalent in earliest historic times, though it is unknown in any lower animal.

The thoughtful dwellers in Farsistan also developed a religion close to man's wants by dividing the gods into those who aid and those who harm him, subject the one class to Ahura-Mazda, the other to Anya-Mainyus. Early in their history this assumed almost a moral aspect, and there is little to be added to one of the most ancient precepts of their law—" Happiness be to the man who conduces to the happiness of all." [1]

When this dual classification sought expression through natural contrasts, there was one which nigh everywhere offered itself as the most appropriate. The savage, the nomad, limited to the utmost in artificial contrivances, met nothing which more signally aided the accom-

[1] This is the first line of Yaçna, 42, of the *Khordah-Avesta*. The Parsees believe that it is the salutation which meets the soul of the good on entering the next world.

plishment of his wishes than *light;* nothing which more certainly frustrated them than *darkness.* From these two sources flow numerous myths, symbols, and rites, as narratives or acts which convey religious thought to the eye or the ear of sense.

As the bringers of light, man adored the sun, the dawn, and fire; associated with warmth and spring, his further meditations saw in it the source of his own and of all life, and led him to connect with its worship that of the reproductive principle. As it comes from above, and seems to dwell in the far-off sky, he located there his good gods, and lifted his hands or his eyes when he prayed. As light is necessary to sight, and as to see is to know, the faculty of knowing was typified as enlightenment, an inward god-given light. The great and beneficent deities are always the gods of light. Their names often show this. Deva, Deus, means the shining one; Michabo, the great white one; the Mongols call Tien, the chief Turanian god, the bright one, the luminous one; the northern Buddhist prays to Amitabha, Infinite Light; and the Christian to the Light of the World.

On the other hand, darkness was connected with feelings of helplessness and terror. It exposed him to attacks of wild beasts and all accidents. It was the precursor of the storm. It was like to death and the grave. The realm of the departed was supposed to be a land of shadows, an underground region, an unseeing Hades or hell.

The task would be easy to show many strange corroborations of these early chosen symbols by the exacter studies of later ages. Light, as the indispensable condition of life, is no dream, but a fact; sight is the highest sentient faculty; and the luminous rays are real intellectual stimulants.[1] But such reflections will not escape the contemplative reader.

I hasten to an important consequence of this dual classification of divinities. It led to what I may call the *quantification of the gods*, that is, to conceiving divinity under notions of number or quantity, a step which has led to profound deterioration of the religious sentiment. I do not mean by this the distinction between polytheism and monotheism. The latter is as untrue and as injurious as the former, nor does it contain a whit the more the real elements of religious progress.

It is indeed singular that this subject has been so misunderstood. Much has been written by Christian theologians to show the superiority of monotheisms; and by their opponents much

---

[1] "Sight is the light sense. Through it we become acquainted with universal relations, this being *reason*. Without the eye there would be no reason." Lorenz Oken, *Elements of Physio-Philosophy*, p. 475.

has been made of Comte's *loi des trois états,* which defines religious progress to be first fetichism, secondly polytheism, finally monotheism. Of this Mr. Lewes says: " The theological system arrived at the highest perfection of which it is capable when it substituted the providential action of a single being, for the varied operations of the numerous divinities which had before been imagined."[1] Nothing could be more erroneous than the spirit of this statement; nothing is more correct, if the ordinary talk of the superiority of monotheism in religion be admitted.

History and long experience show that monotheistic religions have no special good effect either on the morals or the religious sensibility of races.[2] Buddhism,[3] Mohammedanism and Judaism are, at least in theory, uncompromising monotheisms; modern Christianity is less so, as many Catholics pray to the Virgin and Saints, and many Protestants to Christ. So long as *the mathematical conception of number,* whether one or many, is applied to deity by a theological system, it has not yet "arrived at the highest perfection of which it is capable."

For let us inquire what a monotheism is? It

---

[1] *History of Philosophy,* Vol. II. p. 638 (4th ed.)

[2] "The intolerance of almost all religions which have maintained the unity of God, is as remarkable as the contrary principle in polytheism." Hume, *Nat. Hist. of Religion,* Sec. ix.

[3] "The Lamas emphatically maintain monotheism to be the real character of Buddhism." Emil Schlagintweit, *Buddhism in Tibet,* p. 108.

is a belief in one god as distinct from the belief in several gods. In other words, it applies to God the mathematical concept of unity, a concept which can only come into cognition by virtue of contrasts and determinations, and which forces therefore the believer either to Pantheism or anthropomorphism to reconcile his belief with his reason. No other resource is left him. With monotheism there must always be the idea of numerical separateness, which is incompatible with universal conceptions.

Let him, however, clear his mind of the current admiration for monotheisms, and impress upon himself that he who would form a conception of supreme intelligence must do so under the rules of pure thought, not numerical relation. The logical, not the mathematical, unity of the divine is the perfection of theological reasoning. Logical unity does not demand a determination by contrasts; it conveys only the idea of identity with self. As the logical attainment of truth is the recognition of identities in apparent diversity, thus leading from the logically many to the logically one, the assumption of the latter is eminently justified. Every act of reasoning is an additional proof of it.[1]

[1] No one has seen the error here pointed out, and its injurious results on thought, more clearly than Comte himself. He is emphatic in condemning " le tendance involontaire à constituer l'unité spéculative par l'ascendant universel des plus grossières contemplations numérique, géométrique ou mécaniques."

Nor does the duality of nature and thought, to which I have alluded, in any wise contradict this. In pure thought we must understand the dichotomic process to be the distinction of a positive by a privative, both logical elements of the same thought, as I have elsewhere shown. The opposites or contraries referred to as giving rise to the dualistic conceptions of divinity are thus readily harmonized with the conception of logical unity. This was recognized by the Hindoo sage who composed the Bhagavad Gítá, early in our era. Krishna, the Holy One, addressing the King Ardjuna says: "All beings fall into error as to the nature of creation, O Bharata, by reason of that delusion of natural opposites which springs from liking and disliking, oh thou tormentor of thy foes!"[1]

The substitution of the conception of mathematical for logical unity in this connection has left curious traces in both philosophy and religion. It has led to a belief in the triplicate nature of the supreme Being, and to those philosophical triads which have often attracted thinkers, from Pythagoras and Heraclitus down to Hegel and Ghiberti.

Pythagoras, who had thought profoundly on

Système de Politique Positive; Tome I., p. 51. But he was too biassed to apply this warning to Christian thought. The conception of the Universe in the logic of Professor De Morgan and Boole is an example of speculative unity.

[1] *Bhagavad Gítá*, ch. iv.

numbers and their relations, is credited with the obscure maxim that every thought is made up of a definite one and an indefinite two (a μονας and an αοριστος δυας). Some of his commentators have added to rather than lessened the darkness of this saying. But applied to concrete number, it seems clear enough. Take any number, ten, for example, and it is ten by virtue of being a *one*, one ten, and because on either side counting upward or downward, a different number appears, which two are its logical determinants, but, as not expressed, make up an *indefinite two*.

So the number one, thought as concrete unity, is really a trinity, made up of its definite self and its indefinite next greater and lesser determinants. The obscure consciousness of this has made itself felt in many religions when they have progressed to a certain plane of thought. The ancient Egyptian gods were nearly all triune; Phanes, in the Orphic hymns the first principle of things, was tripartite; the Indian trinities are well known; the Celtic triads applied to divine as well as human existence; the Jews distinguished between Jehovah, his Wisdom and his Word; and in Christian religion and philosophy the doctrine of the trinity, though nowhere taught by Christ, has found a lasting foothold, and often presents itself as an actual tritheism.[1]

[1] See the introduction by Mr. J. W. Etheridge to *The Tar-*

The triplicate nature of number, thus alluded to by Pythagoras, springs from the third law of thought, and holds true of all concrete notions. Every such notion stands in necessary relation to its privative, and to the logical concept of next greater extension, *i.e.*, that which includes the notion and its privative, as I explained in the first chapter. This was noted by the early Platonists, who describe a certain concrete expression of it as "the intelligential triad;" and it has been repeatedly commented upon by later philosophers, some of whom avowedly derive from it the proof of the trinitarian dogma as formulated by Athanasius. Even modern mathematical investigations have been supposed to point to a *Deus triformis*, though of course quite another one from that which ancient Rome honored. A late work of much ability makes the statement: "The doctrine of the Trinity, or something analogous to it, forms, as it were, the avenue through which the universe itself leads us up to the conception of the Infinite and Eternal One."[1] The explana-

---

gums *of Onkelos and Jonathan Ben Uzziel* (London, 1862). St. Augustine believed the trinity is referred to in the opening verses of Genesis. *Confessiones*, Lib. xiii. cap. 5. The early Christian writer, Theophilus of Antioch (circa 225), in his *Apologia*, recognizes the Jewish trinity only. It was a century later that the dogma was defined in its Athanasian form. See further, Isaac Preston Cory, *Ancient Fragments, with an Inquiry into the Trinity of the Gentiles* (London, 1832).

[1] *The Unseen Universe*, p. 191.

tion of this notion is the same as that of the "Trinity of the Gentiles," always hitherto a puzzling mythological concept.

For reasons previously given, an analysis of the formal law itself does not yield these elements. They belong to a certain class of values assigned it, not to the law itself; hence it is only when deity is conceived under the conditions of numerical oneness that the tripartite constitution of a whole number makes itself felt, and is applied to the divine nature.

The essence of a logical unit is identity, of a mathematical, difference. The qualities of the latter are limitations—*so much of a thing;* those of the former are coincidences—*that kind of a thing.*

To be sure it is no easy matter to free ourselves from the habit of confounding identity and individuality. We must cultivate a much greater familiarity with the forms of thought, and the character of universals, than every-day life requires of us, before the distinction grows facile. The individual, not the species, exists; our own personality, our thinking faculty is what we are most certain of. On it rests the reality of everything, the Unknown as well. But the rejection of a mathematical unity does not at all depreciate the force of such an argument. Individuality regarded as mathematical unity rests on the deeper law of logical identity from which the validity of numbers rises; it is not the least diminished, but intensified, in the conception of a Supreme Intelligence, as the font of truth, though the confinements and limitations of the mathematical unit fall away, and all contrasts disappear.

The reverse conception, however, has prevailed in religious systems, polytheistic or monotheistic. Man has projected on the cloudy unknown the magnified picture of his own individuality and shuddered with terror at the self-created plantasm, like the peasant frightened by the spectre of the Brocken, formed by the distorted image of himself. In his happier moments, with his hopes gratified, the same vice of thought, still active, prevented him from conceiving any higher ideal than his better self. "Everywhere the same tendency was observed; the gods, always exaggerations of human power and passions, became more and more personifications of what was most admirable and lovable in human nature, till in Christianity there emerged the avowed ideal man." What could it end in but anthropomorphism, or pantheism, or, rejecting both, a Religion of Humanity, with a background of an imbecile Unknowable?

Is it necessary to point out how none of these conclusions can satisfy the enlightened religious sentiment? How anthropomorphism, which makes God in the image of man, instead of acknowledging that man is made in the image of God, belittles divinity to a creature of passions and caprices? How pantheism, increasing God at the expense of man, wipes out the fundamental difference of true and false, calls bad "good in the making," and virtually extinguishes the sense of duty and the permanence of personality? And how the denial of all possible knowledge of the absolute digs away the only foundation on which sanity can establish a religion, and then palms off material comfort as the proper food for religious longing?

The long story of religious effort is not from fetichism to monotheism, as Comte read it; nor is its only possible goal inside the limits of the ego, as Feuerbach and the other Neo-Hegelians assert; but it is on its theoretical side to develope with greater and greater distinctness the unmeasurable reality of pure thought, to dispense more and more with the quantification of the absolute, and to avoid in the representation of that Being the use of the technic of concrete existence.

Little by little we learn that the really true is never true in fact, that the really good is never good in act.[1] Carefully cherishing this distinction taught by mathematics and ethics, the religious mind learns to recognize in that only reality

[1] "A good will is the only altogether good thing in the world."
—*Kant.* "What man conceives in himself is always superior to that reality which it precedes and prepares."—*Comte.*

darkly seen through the glass of material things, that which should fix and fill its meditations. Passing beyond the domain of physical law, it occupies itself with that which defines the conditions of law. It contemplates an eternal activity, before which its own self-consciousness seems a flickering shadow, yet in that contemplation is not lost but gains an evergrowing personality.

This is the goal of religious striving, the hidden aim of the wars and persecutions, the polemics and martyrdoms, which have so busied and bloodied the world. This satisfies the rational postulates of religion. Does some one say that it does not stimulate its emotional elements, that it does not supply the impulses of action which must ever be the criteria of the true faith? Is it not a religion at all, but a philosophy, a search, or if you prefer, a love for the truth?

Let such doubter ponder well the signification of truth, its relation to life, its identity with the good, and the paramount might of wisdom and a clear understanding, and he will be ready to exclaim with the passionate piety of St. Augustine: "*Ubi inveni veritatem, ibi inveni Deum meum, ipsam veritatem, quam, ex quo didici, non sum oblitus.*"

From this brief review of its character, the Myth will be seen to be one of the transitory expressions of the religious sentiment, which in enlightened lands it has already outgrown and should lay aside. So far as it relates to events, real or alleged, historic or geologic, it deals with that which is indifferent to pure religion; and so far as it assumes to reveal the character, plans and temper of divinity, it is too evidently a reflex of man's personality to be worthy of serious refutation where it conflicts with the better guide he has within him.

THE CULT, ITS SYMBOLS AND RITES.

SUMMARY.

The Symbol represents the unknown; the Rite is the ceremony of worship.

A symbol stands for the supernatural, an emblem for something known. The elucidation of symbolism is in the laws of the association of ideas. Associations of similarity give related symbols, of contiguity coincident symbols. Symbols tend either toward personification (iconolatry), or toward secularization. The symbol has no fixed interpretation. Its indefiniteness shown by the serpent symbol, and the cross. The physiological relations of certain symbols. Their classification. The Lotus. The Pillar. Symbols discarded by the higher religious thought. Esthetic and scientific symbolism (the "Doctrine of Correspondences").

Rites are either propitiatory or memorial. The former spring either from the idea of sacrifice or of specific performance. A sacrifice is a gift, but its measure is what it costs the giver. Specific performance means that a religious act should have no ulterior aim. Vicarious sacrifice and the idea of sin.

Memorial rites are intended to recall the myth, or else to keep up the organization. The former are dramatic or imitative, the latter institutionary. Tendency of memorial rites to become propitiatory. Examples.

CHAPTER VI.

THE CULT, ITS SYMBOLS AND RITES.

As the side which a religious system presents to the intellect is shown in the Myth, so the side that it presents to sense is exhibited in the Cult. This includes the representation and forms of worship of the unknown power which presides over the fruition of the Prayer or religious wish. The representation is effected by the Symbol, the worship by the Rite. The development of these two, and their relation to religious thought, will be the subject of the present chapter.

The word Symbolism has a technical sense in theological writings, to wit, the discussion of creeds, quite different from that in which it is used in mythological science. Here it means the discussion of the natural objects which have been used to represent to sense supposed supernatural beings. As some conception of such beings must first be formed, the symbol is necessarily founded upon the myth, and must be explained by it.

A symbol is closely allied to an emblem, the distinction being that the latter is intended to represent some abstract conception or concrete fact, not supposed to be supernatural. Thus the serpent is the emblem of Esculapius, or, abstractly, of the art of healing; but in its use as a symbol in Christian art it stands for the Evil One, a supernatural being. The heraldric insignia of the Middle Ages were emblematic devices; but the architecture of the cathedrals was largely symbolic. Both agree in aiming to aid the imagination and the memory, and both may appeal to any special sense, although the majority are addressed to sight alone.

Symbolism has not received the scientific treatment which has been so liberally bestowed on mythology. The first writer who approached it in the proper spirit was Professor Creuzer.[1] Previous to his labors the distinction between pictographic and symbolic art was not well defined. He drew the line sharply, and illustrated it abundantly; but he did not preserve so clearly the relations of the symbol and the myth. Indeed, he regarded the latter as a symbol, a "phonetic" one, to be treated by the same pro-

[1] In his chapter *Ideen zu einer Physik des Symbols und des Mythus*, of his *Symbolik und Mythologie*.

cesses of analysis. Herein later students have not consented to follow him. The contrast between these two expressions of the religious sentiment becomes apparent when we examine their psychological origin. This Professor Creuzer did not include in his researches, nor is it dwelt upon at any length in the more recent works on the subject.[1] The neglect to do this has given rise to an arbitrariness in the interpretation of many symbols, which has often obscured their position in religious history.

What these principles are I shall endeavor to indicate; and first of the laws of the origin of symbols, the rules which guided the early intellect in choosing from the vast number of objects appealing to sense those fit to shadow forth the supernatural.

It may safely be assumed that this was not done capriciously, as the modern parvenue makes for himself a heraldric device. The simple and devout intellect of the primitive man imagined a real connection between the god and the symbol. Were this questioned, yet the wonderful unanimity with which the same natural objects, the serpent, the bird, the tree, for example, were everywhere chosen, proves that their selection was not the work of chance. The constant preference of these objects points conclusively to

[1] Dr. H. C. Barlow's *Essays on Symbolism* (London, 1866), deserves mention as one of the best of these.

some strong and frequent connection of their images with mythical concepts.

The question of the origin of symbols therefore resolves itself into one of the association of ideas, and we start from sure ground in applying to their interpretation the established canons of association. These, as I have elsewhere said, are those of contiguity and similarity, the former producing association by the closeness of succession of impressions or thoughts, the latter through impressions or thoughts recalling like ones in previous experience. When the same occurrence affects different senses simultaneously, or nearly so, the association is one of *contiguity*, as thunder and lightning, for a sound cannot be *like* a sight; when the same sense is affected in such a manner as to recall a previous impression, the association is one of *similarity*, as when the red autumn leaves recall the hue of sunset. Nearness in time or nearness in kind is the condition of association.

The intensity or permanence of the association depends somewhat on temperament, but chiefly on repetition or continuance. Not having an ear for music, I may find it difficult to recall a song from hearing its tune; but by dint of frequent repetition I learn to associate them. Light and heat, smoke and fire, poverty and hunger so frequently occur together, that the one is apt to recall the other. So do a large number of antithetical associations, as light and darkness, heat and cold, by *inverse similarity*, opposite impressions reviving each other, in accordance with the positive and privative elements of a notion.

This brief reference to the laws of applied thought,—too brief, did I not take for granted that they are generally familiar—furnishes the clue to guide us through the labyrinth of symbolism, to wit, the repeated association of the event or power recorded in the myth with some sensuous image. Where there is a connection in kind between the symbol and that for which it stands, there is *related* symbolism; where the connection is one of juxtaposition in time, there is *coincident* symbolism. Mother Earth, fertile and fecund, was a popular deity in many nations, and especially among the Egyptians, who worshipped her under the symbol of a cow; this is related symbolism; the historical event of the execution of Christ occurred by crucifixion, one of several methods common in that age, and since then the cross has been the symbol of Christianity; this is coincident symbolism. It is easy for the two to merge, as when the cross was identified with a somewhat similar and much older symbol, one of the class I have called "related," signifying the reproductive principle, and became the "tree of life." As a coincident symbol is to a certain extent accidental in origin, related symbols have always been most agreeable to the religious sentiment.

This remark embodies the explanation of the growth of religious symbolism, and also its gradual decay into decorative art and mnemonic design. The tendency of related symbolism is toward the identification of the symbol with that for which it stands, toward personification or prosopopeia; while what I may call the *secularization* of symbols is brought about by regarding them more and more as accidental connections, by giving them conventional forms, and treating them as elements of architectural or pictorial design, or as aids to memory.

This tendency of related symbolism depends on a law of applied thought which has lately been formulated by a distinguished logician in the following words: "What is true of a thing, is true of its like."[1] The similarity of the symbol to its prototype assumed, the qualities of the symbol, even those which had no share in deciding its selection, no likeness to the original, were lumped, and transferred to the divinity. As those like by similarity, so those unlike, were identified by contiguity, as traits of the unknown power. This is the active element in the degeneracy of religious idealism. The cow or the bull, chosen first as a symbol of creation

[1] W. S. Jevons, *The Substitution of Similars*, p. 15 (London, 1869.)

or fecundity, led to a worship of the animal itself, and a transfer of its traits, even to its horns, to the god. In a less repulsive form, the same tendency shows itself in the pietistic ingenuity of such poets as Adam de Sancto Victore and George Herbert, who delight in taking some biblical symbol, and developing from it a score of applications which the original user never dreamt of. In such hands a chance simile grows to an elaborate myth.

Correct thought would prevent the extension of the value of the symbol beyond the original element of similarity. More than this, it would recognize the fact that similarity does not suppose identity, but the reverse, to wit, defect of likeness; and this dissimilitude must be the greater, as the original and symbol are naturally discrepant. The supernatual, however, whether by this term we mean the unknown or the universal—still more if we mean the incomprehensible—is utterly discrepant with the known, except by an indefinitely faint analogy. In the higher thought, therefore, the symbol loses all trace of identity and becomes merely emblematic.

The ancients defended symbolic teaching on this very ground, that the symbol left so much unexplained, that it stimulated the intellect and trained it to profounder thinking;[1] practically

[1] Creuzer, *Symbolik*, Bd. I., s. 59.

it had the reverse effect, the symbol being accepted as the thing itself.

Passing from these general rules of the selection of symbols, to the history of the symbol when chosen, this presents itself to us in a reciprocal form, first as the myth led to the adoption and changes in the symbol, and as the latter in turn altered and reformed the myth.

The tropes and figures of rhetoric by which the conceptions of the supernatural were first expressed, give the clue to primitive symbolism. A very few examples will be sufficient. No one can doubt that the figure of the serpent was sometimes used in pictorial art to represent the lightning, when he reads that the Algonkins *straightly* called the latter a snake; when he sees the same adjective, spiral or winding, (ἑλικοειδής) applied by the Greeks to the lightning and a snake; when the Quiché call the electric flash a strong serpent; and many other such examples. The Pueblo Indians represent lightning in their pictographs by a zigzag line. A zigzag fence is called in the Middle States a worm or "snake" fence. Besides this, adjectives which describe the line traced by the serpent in motion are applied to many twisting or winding objects, as a river, a curl or lock of hair, the tendrils of a vine, the intestines, a trailing plant, the mazes of a dance, a bracelet, a broken ray of light, a sickle, a crooked limb, an anfractuous path, the phallus, etc. Hence the figure of a serpent may, and in fact has been, used with direct reference to every one of these, as could easily be shown. How short-sighted then the expounder of symbolism who would explain the frequent recurrence of the symbol or the myth of the serpent wherever he finds it by any one of these!

This narrowness of exposition becomes doubly evident when we give consideration to two other elements in primitive symbolism—the multivocal nature of early designs, and the misapprehensions due to contiguous association.

To illustrate the first, let us suppose, with Schwarz[1] and others, that the serpent was at first the symbol of the lightning. Its most natural representation would be in motion; it might then stand for the other serpentine objects I have mentioned; but once accepted as an acknowledged symbol, the other qualities and properties of the serpent would present themselves to the mind, and the effort would be made to discover or to imagine likenesses to these in the electric flash. The serpent is venomous; it casts its skin and thus seems to renew its life; it is said to fascinate its prey; it lives in the ground; it hisses or rattles when disturbed: none of these properties is present to the mind of the savage who scratches on the rock a zigzag line to represent the lightning god. But after-thought brings

[1] *Ursprung der Mythologie* (Berlin, 1862).

them up, and the association of contiguity can apply them all to the lightning, and actually has done so over and over again; and not only to it, but also to other objects originally represented by a broken line, for example, the river gods and the rays of light.

This complexity is increased by the ambiguous representation of symbolic designs. The serpent, no longer chosen for its motion alone, will be expressed in art in that form best suited to the meaning of the symbol present in the mind of the artist. Realism is never the aim of religious art. The zigzag line, the coil, the spiral, the circle and the straight line, are all geometrical radicals of various serpentine forms. Any one of these may be displayed with fanciful embellishments and artistic aids. Or the artist, proceeding by synecdoche, takes a part for the whole, and instead of portraying the entire animal, contents himself with one prominent feature or one aspect of it. A striking instance of this has been developed by Dr. Harrison Allen, in the prevalence of what he calls the "crotalean curve," in aboriginal American art, a line which is the radical of the profile view of the head of the rattlesnake (*crotalus*).[1] This he has detected in the architectural monuments of Mexico and Yucatan, in the Maya phonetic scrip, and even in the rude efforts of the savage tribes. Each of these elective methods of repre-

---

[1] Harrison Allen, M. D., *The Life Form in Art*, Phila. 1874.

senting the serpent, would itself, by independent association, call up ideas out of all connection whatever with that which the figure first symbolized. These, in the mind entertaining them, will supersede and efface the primitive meaning. Thus the circle is used in conventional symbolic art to designate the serpent; but also the eye, the ear, the open mouth, the mamma, the sun, the moon, a wheel, the womb, the vagina, the return of the seasons, time, continued life, hence health, and many other things. Whichever of these ideas is easiest recalled will first appear on looking at a circle. The error of those who have discussed mythological symbolism has been to trace a connection of such adventitious ideas beyond the symbol to its original meaning; whereas the symbol itself is the starting-point. To one living in a region where venomous serpents abound, the figure of one will recall the sense of danger, the dread of the bite, and the natural hostility we feel to those who hurt us; whereas no such ideas would occur to the native of a country where there are no snakes, or where they are harmless, unless taught this association.

Few symbols have received more extended study than that of the cross, owing to its prominence in Christian art. This, as I have said, was coincident or incidental only. It corresponded, however, to a current "phonetic symbol," in the expression common to the Greeks and

Romans of that day, "to take up one's cross," meaning to prepare for the worst, a metaphor used by Christ himself.

Now there is no agreement as to what was the precise form of the cross on which he suffered. Three materially unlike crosses are each equally probable. In symbolic art these have been so multiplied that now *two hundred and twenty-two* variants of the figure are described![1] Of course there is nothing easier than to find among these similarities, with many other conventional symbols, the Egyptian Tau, the Hammer of Thor, the " Tree of Fertility," on which the Aztecs nailed their victims, the crossed lines which are described on Etruscan tombs, or the logs crossed at rectangles, on which the Muskogee Indians built the sacred fire. The four cardinal points are so generally objects of worship, that more than any other mythical conception they have been represented by cruciform figures. But to connect these in any way with the symbol as it appears in Christian art, is to violate every scientific principle.

Each variant of a symbol may give rise to myths quite independent of its original meaning. A symbol once adopted is preserved by its sacred character, exists long as a symbol, but with ever fluctuating significations. It always takes that which is uppermost in the mind of the votary and

[1] Cussans, *Grammar of Heraldry*, p. 16.

the congregation. Hence, psychology, and especially the psychology of races, is the only true guide in symbolic exegesis.

Nor is the wide adoption and preservation of symbols alone due to an easily noticed similarity between certain objects and the earliest conceptions of the supernatural, or to the preservative power of religious veneration.

I have previously referred to the associations of ideas arising from ancestral reversions of memory, and from the principles of minimum muscular action and harmonic excitation. Such laws make themselves felt unconsciously from the commencement of life, with greater or less power, dependent on the susceptibility of the nervous system. They go far toward explaining the recurrence and permanence of symbols, whether of sight or sound. Thus I attribute the prevalence of the serpentine curve in early religious art largely to its approach to the " line of beauty," which is none other than that line which the eye, owing to the arrangement of its muscles, can follow with the minimum expenditure of nervous energy. The satisfaction of the mind in viewing symmetrical figures or harmonious coloring, as also that of the ear, in hearing accordant sounds, is, as I have remarked, based on the principle of maximum action with minimum waste. The mind gets the most at the least cost.

The equilateral triangle, which is the simplest geometrical figure which can enclose a space, thus satisfying the mind the easiest of any, is nigh universal in symbolism. It is seen in the Egyptian pyramids, whose sides are equilateral triangles with a common apex, in the mediæval cathedrals, whose designs are combinations of such triangles, in the sign for the trinity, the pentalpha, etc.

The classification of some symbols of less extensive prevalence must be made from their phonetic values. One class was formed as were the "canting arms" in heraldry, that is, by a rebus. This is in its simpler form, direct, as when Quetzalcoatl, the mystical hero-god of Atzlan, is represented by a bird on a serpent, *quetzal* signifying a bird, *coatl* a serpent; or composite, two or more of such rebus symbols being blended by synecdoche, like the "marshalling" of arms in heraldry, as when the same god is portrayed by a feathered serpent; or the rebus may occur with paronymy, especially when the literal meaning of a name of the god is lost, as when the Algonkins forgot the sense of the word *wabish*, white or bright, as applied to their chief divinity, and confounding it with *wabos*, a rabbit, wove various myths about their ancestor, the Great Hare, and chose the hare or rabbit as a totemic badge.[1]

---

[1] Numerous examples from classical antiquity are given by Creuzer, *Symbolik*, Bd. i. s. 114. sqq.

It is almost needless to add further that the ideas most frequently associated with the unknown object of religion are those, which, struggling after material expression, were most fecund in symbols. We have but to turn to the Orphic hymns, or those of the Vedas or the Hebrew Psalms, to see how inexhaustible was the poetic fancy, stirred by religious awe, in the discovery of similitudes, any of which, under favoring circumstances, might become a symbol.

Before leaving this branch of my subject, I may illustrate some of the preceding comments by applying them to one or two well known subjects of religious art.

A pleasing symbol, which has played a conspicuous part in many religions, is the Egyptian lotus, or "lily of the Nile." It is an aquatic plant, with white, roseate or blue flowers, which float upon the water, and send up from their centre long stamens. In Egypt it grows with the rising of the Nile, and as its appearance was coincident with that important event, it came to take prominence in the worship of Isis and Osiris as the symbol of fertility. Their mystical marriage took place in its blossom. In the technical language of the priests, however, it bore a profounder meaning, that of the supremacy of reason above matter, the contrast being between the beautiful flower and the muddy water which bears it.[1] In India the lotus bears other and manifold meanings. It is a symbol of the sacred river Ganges, and of the morally pure. No prayer in the world has ever been more frequently repeated than this: "Om! the jewel in the lotus. Amen" (*om mani padme hum*). Many millions of times, every hour, for centuries, has this been iterated by the Buddhists of Thibet and the countries north of it. What it means, they can only explain by fantastic and mystical guesses. Probably it refers to the legendary birth of their chief saint, Avalokitesvara, who is said to have been born of a lotus flower. But some say it is a piece of symbolism not strange to its meaning in Egypt,[2] and borrowed by Buddhism from the Siva worship. In the symbolic language of this sect the lotus is the symbol of the vagina, while the phallus is called "the jewel." With this interpretation the Buddhist prayer would refer to the reproductive act; but it is illustrative of the necessity of attributing wholly diverse meanings to the same symbol, that the Buddhists neither now nor at any past time attached any such signification to the expression, and it would be most discrepant with their doctrines to do so.[3]

[1] W. von Humboldt, *Gesammelte Werke*, Bd. iv., s. 332.

[2] Creuzer, *Symbolik und Mythologie*, Bd. i., s. 282.

[3] Carl Frederick Koppen, *Die Lamaische Hierarchie and Kirche*, ss. 59, 60, 61.

Another symbol has frequently been open to this duplicate interpretation, that is, the upright pillar. The Egyptian obelisk, the pillars of "Irmin" or of "Roland," set up now of wood, now of stone by the ancient Germans, the "red-painted great warpole" of the American Indians, the May-pole of Old England, the spire of sacred edifices, the staff planted on the grave, the terminus of the Roman landholders, all these objects have been interpreted to be symbols of life, or the life-force. As they were often of wood, the trunk of a tree for instance, they have often been called by titles equivalent to the "tree of life," and are thus connected with the nigh innumerable myths which relate to some mystic tree as the source of life. The ash Ygdrasyl of the Edda, the oak of Dordona and of the Druid, the modern Christmas tree, the sacred banyan, the holy groves, illustrate but faintly the prevalence of tree worship. Even so late as the time of Canute, it had to be forbidden in England by royal edict.

Now, the general meaning of this symbol I take to be the same as that which led to the choice of hills and "high places," as sites for altars and temples, and to the assigning of mountain tops as the abodes of the chief gods. It is seen in adjectives applied, I believe, in all languages, certainly all developed ones, to such deities themselves. These adjectives are related to adverbs of place, signifying *above*, *up* or *over*. We speak of the supernatural, or supernal powers, the Supreme Being, the Most High, He in Heaven, and such like. So do all Aryan and Semitic tongues. Beyond them, the Chinese name for the Supreme Deity, Tien, means *up*. I have elsewhere illustrated the same fact in native American tongues. The association of light and the sky above, the sun and the heaven, is why we raise our hands and eyes in confident prayer to divinity. That at times, however, a religion of sex-love did identify these erect symbols with the phallus as the life-giver, is very true, but this was a temporary and adventitious meaning assigned a symbol far more ancient than this form of religion.

In this review of the principles of religious symbolism, I have attempted mainly to exhibit the part it has sustained in the development of the religious sentiment. It has been generally unfavorable to the growth of higher thought. The symbol, in what it is above the emblem, assumes more than a similarity, a closer relation than analogy; to some degree it pretends to a hypostatic union or identity of the material with the divine, the known to sense with the unknown. Fully seen, this becomes object worship; partially so, personification.

There is no exception to this. The refined symbolisms which pass current to day as religious philosophies exemplify it. The one, esthetic symbolism, has its field in musical and architectural art, in the study and portraiture of the beautiful; the other, scientific symbolism, claims to discover in the morphology of organisms, in the harmonic laws of physics, and in the processes of the dialectic, the proof that symbolism, if not a revelation, is at least an unconscious inspiration of universal truth. This is the "Doctrine of Correspondences," much in favor with Swedenborgians, but by no means introduced by the founder of that sect. The recognition of the identity in form of the fundamental laws of motion and thought, and the clearer understanding of the character of harmony which the experiments of Helmholtz and others give us, disperse most of the mystery about these similarities. The religion of art, as such, will come up for consideration in the next chapter.

The second form of the Cult is the Rite. This includes the acts or ceremonies of worship. Considered in the gross, they can be classed as of two kinds, the first and earliest propitiatory, the second and later memorial or institutionary.

We have but to bear in mind the one aspiration of commencing religious thought, to wit, the attainment of a wish, to see that whatever action arose therefrom must be directed to that purpose. Hence, when we analyze the rude ceremonies of savage cults, the motive is extremely apparent. They, like their prayers, all point to the securing of some material advantage. They are designed

> "to cozen
> The gods that constrain us and curse."

The motives which underlie these simplest as well as the most elaborate rituals, and impress upon them their distinctively religious character can be reduced to two, the idea of *sacrifice* and the idea of *specific performance*.

The simplest notion involved in a sacrifice is that of *giving*. The value of the gift is not, however, the intrinsic worth of the thing given, nor even the pleasure or advantage the recipient derives therefrom, but, singularly enough, the amount of pain the giver experiences in depriving himself of it! This is also often seen in ordinary transactions. A rich man who subscribes a hundred dollars to a charity, is thought to merit less commendation than the widow who gives her mite. Measured by motive, this reasoning is correct. There is a justice which can be vindicated in holding self-denial to be a standard of motive. All developed religions have demanded the renunciation of what is dearest. The Ynglyngasaga tells us that in a time of famine, the first sacrifice offered to the gods was of beasts only; if this failed, men were slain to appease them; and if this did not mitigate their anger, the king himself was obliged to die that they might send plenty. The Latin writers have handed it down that among the Germans and Gauls a human sacrifice was deemed the more efficacious the more distinguished the victim, and the nearer his relationship to him who offered the rite.[1] The slaughter of children and wives to please the gods was common in many religions, and the self-emasculation of the priests of Cybele, with other such painful rites, indicates that the measure of the sacrifice was very usually not what the god needed, but the willingness of the worshipper to give.

The second idea, that of *specific performance*, has been well expressed and humorously commented upon by Hume in his *Natural History of Religions*. He says: " Here I cannot forbear observing a fact which may be worth the attention of those who make human nature the object of their inquiry. It is certain that in every religion, many of the votaries, perhaps the greatest number, will seek the divine favor, not by virtue and good morals, but either by frivolous observances, by intemperate zeal, by rapturous ecstasies, or by the belief of mysterious and absurd opinions. * * * In all this [*i. e.*, in virtue and good morals], a superstitious man finds nothing, which he has properly performed for the sake of his deity, or

[1] Adolph Holtzmann, *Deutsche Mythologie*, p. 232 (Leipzig, 1874).

which can peculiarly recommend him to divine favor and protection. * * * * But if he fast or give himself a sound whipping, this has a direct reference, in his opinion, to the service of God. No other motive could engage him to such austerities."

The philosopher here sets forth in his inimitable style a marked characteristic of religious acts. But he touches upon it with his usual superficiality. It is true that no religion has ever been content with promoting the happiness of man, and that the vast majority of votaries are always seeking to do something specifically religious, and are not satisfied with the moral only. The simple explanation of it is that the religious sentiment has a purpose entirely distinct from ethics, a purpose constantly felt as something peculiar to itself, though obscurely seen and often wholly misconceived. It is only when an action is utterly dissevered from other ends, and is purely and solely religious, that it can satisfy this sentiment. "*La religion*," most truly observes Madame Necker de Saussure, "*ne doit point avoir d'autre but qu'elle même.*"

The uniform prevalence of these ideas in rites may be illustrated from the simplest or the most elaborate. Father Brebeuf, missionary to the Hurons in 1636, has a chapter on their superstitions. He there tells us that this nation had two sorts of ceremonies, the one to induce the gods to grant good fortune, the other to appease them when some ill-luck had occurred. Before running a dangerous rapid in their frail canoes they would lay tobacco on a certain rock where the deity of the rapid was supposed to reside, and ask for safety in their voyage. They took tobacco and cast it in the fire, saying: "O Heaven (*Aronhiaté*), see, I give you something; aid me; cure this sickness of mine." When one was drowned or died of cold, a feast was called, and the soft parts of the corpse were cut from the bones and burned to conciliate the personal god, while the women danced and chanted a melancholy strain. Here one sacrifice was to curry favor with the gods, another to soothe their anger, and the third was a rite, not a sacrifice, but done for a religious end, whose merit was specific performance.

As the gift was valued at what it cost the giver, and was supposed to be efficacious in this same ratio, self-denial soon passed into self-torture, prolonged fasts, scourging and lacerations, thus becoming legitimate exhibitions of religious fervor. As mental pain is as keen as bodily pain, the suffering of Jephthah was quite as severe as that of the Flagellants, and was expected to find favor in the eyes of the gods.

A significant corrollary from such a theory follows: that which is the efficacious part of the sacrifice is the suffering; given a certain degree of this, the desired effect will follow. As to what or who suffers, or in what manner he or it suffers, these are secondary considerations, even unimportant ones, so far as the end to be obtained is concerned. This is the germ of *vicarious* sacrifice, a plan frequently observed in even immature religions. What seems the diabolical cruelty of some superstitious rites, those of the Carthaginians and Celts, for example, is thoroughly consistent with the abstract theory of sacrifice, and did not spring from capricious malice. The Death of Christ, regarded as a general vicarious atonement, has had its efficiency explained directly by the theory that the pain he suffered partook of the infinity of his divine nature; as thus it was excruciating beyond measure, so it was infinitely effectual toward appeasing divinity.

It is well known that this doctrine was no innovation on the religious sentiment of the age when it was preached by the Greek fathers. For centuries the Egyptian priests had taught the incarnation and sufferings of Osiris, and his death for the salvation of his people. Similar myths were common throughout the Orient, all drawn from the reasoning I have mentioned.[1]

They have been variously criticized. Apart

---

[1] "Es ist so gewissermassen in allen ernsten orientalischen Lehren das Christenthum in seinem Keime vorgebildet." Creuzer, *Symbolik und Mythologie der Alten Völker*, Bd. i., s. 297.

from the equivocal traits this theory of atonement attributes to the supernatural powers—a feature counterbalanced, in modern religion, by subduing its harshest features—it is rooted essentially in the material view of religion. The religious value of an act is to be appraised by the extent to which it follows recognition of duty. To acknowledge an error is unpleasant; to renounce it still more so, for it breaks a habit; to see our own errors in their magnitude, sullying our whole nature and reaching far ahead to generations yet unborn, is consummately bitter, and in proportion as it is bitter, will keep us from erring.[1] This is the "sacrifice of a contrite heart," which alone is not despicable; and this no one can do for us. We may be sure that neither the physical pain of victims burning in a slow fire, nor the mental pain of yielding up whatever we hold dearest upon earth, will make our views of duty a particle clearer or our notion of divinity a jot nobler; and whatever does neither of these is not of true religion.

The theory of sacrifice is intimately related with the idea of sin. In the quotation I have made from Father Brebeuf we see that the

[1] In a conversation reported by Mr. John Morley, John Stuart Mill expressed his belief that "the coming modification of religion" will be controlled largely through men becoming "more and more impressed with the awful fact that a piece of conduct to-day may prove a curse to men and women scores and even hundreds of years after the author of it is dead."

Hurons recognized a distinct form of rite as appropriate to appease a god when angered. It is a matter of national temperament which of these forms takes the lead. Joutel tells of a tribe in Texas who paid attention only to the gods who worked them harm, saying that the good gods were good anyhow. By parity of reasoning, one sect of Mohammedans worship the devil only. It is well to make friends with your enemy, and then he will not hurt you; and if a man is shielded from his enemies, he is safe enough.

But where, as in most Semitic, Celtic and various other religions, the chief gods frowned or smiled as they were propitiated or neglected, and when a certain amount of pain was the propitiation they demanded, the necessity of rendering this threw a dark shadow on life. What is the condition of man, that only through sorrow he can reach joy? He must be under a curse.

Physical and mental processes aided by analogy this gloomy deduction. It is only through pain that we are stimulated to the pursuit of pleasure, and the latter is a phantom we never catch. The laws of correct reasoning are those which alone should guide us; but the natural laws of the association of ideas do not at all correspond with the one association which reason accepts. Truth is what we are born for, error is what is given us.

Instead of viewing this state of things as one inseparable to the relative as another than the universal, and, instead of seeing the means of correcting it in the mental element of attention, continuance or volition, guided by experience and the growing clearness of the purposes of the laws of thought, the problem was given up as hopeless, and man was placed under a ban from which a god alone could set him free; he was sunk in original sin, chained to death.

To reach this result it is evident that a considerable effort at reasoning, a peculiar view of the nature of the gods, and a temperament not the most common, must be combined. Hence it was adopted as a religious dogma by but a few nations. The Chinese know nothing of the "sense of sin," nor did the Greeks and Romans. The Parsees do not acknowledge it, nor do the American tribes. "To sin," in their languages, does not mean to offend the deity, but to make a mistake, to miss the mark, to loose one's way as in a wood, and the missionaries have exceeding difficulty in making them understand the theological signification of the word.

The second class of rites are memorial in character. As the former were addressed to the gods, so these are chiefly for the benefit of the people. They are didactic, to preserve the myth, or institutionary, to keep alive the discipline and forms of the church.

Of this class of rites it may broadly be said they are the myth dramatized. Indeed, the drama owes its origin to the mimicry by worshippers of the supposed doings of the gods. The most ancient festivals have reference to the recurrence of the seasons, and the ceremonies which mark them represent the mythical transactions which are supposed to govern the yearly changes. The god himself was often represented by the high priest, and masked figures took the parts of attendant deities.

Institutionary rites are those avowedly designed to commemorate a myth or event, and to strengthen thereby the religious organization. Christian baptism is by some denominations looked upon as a commemorative or institutionary rite only; and the same is the case with the Lord's Supper. These seem to have been the only rites recommended, though the former was not practiced by Christ. In any ordinary meaning of his words, he regarded them both as institutionary.

The tendency of memorial to become propitiatory rites is visible in all materialistic religions. The procedure, from a simple commemorative act, acquires a mystic efficacy, a supernatural or spiritual power, often supposed to extend to the deity as well as the votary. Thus the Indian "rain-maker" will rattle his gourd, beat his drum, and blow through his pipe, to represent the thunder, lightning, and wind of the storm; and he believes that by this mimicry of the rain-god's proceedings he can force him to send the wished-for showers. The charms, spells and incantations of sorcery have the same foundation. Equally visible is it in the reception of the Christian rites above mentioned, baptism and the Eucharist, as "sacraments," as observances of divine efficacy in themselves. All such views arise from the material character of the religious wants.

The conclusion is that, while emblems and memorial rites have nothing in them which can mar, they also have nothing which can aid the growth and purity of the religious sentiment, beyond advancing its social relations; while symbols, in the proper sense of the term, and propitiatory rites, as necessarily false and without foundation, always degrade and obscure religious thought. Their prominence in a cult declines, as it rises in quality; and in a perfected scheme of worship they would have no place whatever.

THE MOMENTA OF RELIGIOUS THOUGHT.

SUMMARY.

National impulses and aims as historic ideas. Their recurrence and its explanation. Their permanence in relation to their truth and consciousness. The historic ideas in religious progress are chiefly three.

I. The Idea of the Perfected Individual.

First placed in physical strength. This gave way in Southern Europe to the idea of physical symmetry, a religion of beauty and art. Later days have produced the idea of mental symmetry, the religion of culture. All have failed, and why? The momenta of true religion in each.

II. The Idea of the Perfected Commonwealth.

Certain national temperaments predispose to individualism, others to communism. The social relations governed at first by divine law. Later, morality represents this law. The religion of conduct. The religion of sentiment and of humanity. Advantages and disadvantages in this idea.

Comparisons of these two ideas as completed respectively by Wilhelm von Humboldt and Auguste Comte.

III. The Idea of Personal Survival.

The doctrine of immortality the main moment in Christianity, Islam and Buddhism. Unfamiliar to old and simple faiths. Its energy and speculative relations. It is decreasing as a religious moment owing to, (1) a better understanding of ethics, (2) more accurate cosmical conceptions, (3) the clearer defining of life, (4) the increasing immateriality of religions.

The future and final moments of religious thought.

CHAPTER VII.

THE MOMENTA OF RELIGIOUS THOUGHT.

The records of the past can be studied variously. Events can be arranged in the order of their occurrence : this is chronology or annals ; in addition to this, their connections and mutual relations as cause and effect may be shown : this is historical science ; or, thirdly, from a general view of trains of related events some abstract aim as their final cause may be theoretically deduced and confirmed by experience : this is the philosophy of history. The doctrine of final causes, in its old form as the *argumentum de appetitu*, has been superseded. Function is not purpose ; desire comes from the experience of pleasure, and realizes its dreams, if at all, by the slow development of capacity. The wish carries no warrant of gratification with it. No " argument from design " can be adduced from the region where the laws of physical necessity prevail. Those laws are not designed for an end.

When, however, in the unfolding of mind we reach the stage of notions, we observe a growing power to accomplish desire, not only by altering the individual or race organism, but also by bringing external objects into unison with the desire, reversing the process common in the life of sensation. This spectacle, however, is confined to man alone, and man as guided by prospective volition, that is, by an object ahead.

When some such object is common to a nation or race, it exercises a wide influence on its destiny, and is the key to much that otherwise would be inexplicable in its actions. What we call national hopes, ambitions and ideals are such objects. Sometimes they are distinctly recognized by the nation, sometimes they are pursued almost unconsciously. They do not correspond to things as they are, but as they are wished to be. Hence there is nothing in them to insure their realization. They are like an appetite, which may and may not develope the function which can gratify it. They have been called "historic ideas," and their consideration is a leading topic in modern historical science.

Reason claims the power of criticizing such ideas, and of distinguishing in them between what is true and therefore obtainable, and what is false and therefore chimerical or even destructive. This is the province of the philosophy of history. It guides itself by those general principles for the pursuit of truth which have been noticed in brief in the earlier pages of this book. Looking before as well as after, it aspires in the united light of experience and the laws of mind, to construct for the race an ideal within the reach of its capacities, yet which will develope them to the fullest extent, a pole-star to which it can trust in this night teeming with will-o'-the wisps.

The opinion that the history of mind is a progress whose end will be worth more than was its beginning, may not prove true in fact—the concrete expression never wholly covers the abstract requirements—but it is undoubtedly true in theory. The progress, so far, has been by no means a lineal one—each son a better man than his father—nor even, as some would have it, a spiral one—periodical recurrences to the same historical ideas, but each recurrence a nearer approach to the philosophical idea—but it has been far more complex and irregular than any geometrical figure will illustrate. These facile generalizations do not express it.

Following the natural laws of thought man has erred infinitely, and his errors have worked their sure result — they have destroyed him. There is no "relish of salvation" in an error; otherwise than that it is sure to kill him who obstructs the light by harboring it. There is no sort of convertability of the false into the true, as shallow thinkers of the day teach.

Man has only escaped death when at first by a lucky chance, and then by personal and inherited experience, his thoughts drifted or were forced into conformity with the logical laws of thought.

A historic idea is a complex product formed of numerous conceptions, some true and others false. Its permanency and efficacy are in direct proportion to the number and clearness of the former it embraces. When it is purging itself of the latter, the nation is progressive; when the false are retained, their poison spreads and the nation decays.

The *periodical recurrence* of historic ideas is one of their most striking features. The explanations offered for it have been various. The ancient doctrines of an exact repetition of events in the cycles of nature, and of the transmigration of souls, drew much support from it; and the modern modification of the latter theory as set forth by Wordsworth and Lessing, are distinctly derived from the same source. Rightly elucidated, the philosophical historian will find in it an invaluable clue to the unravelment of the tangled skein of human endeavor.

Historic periodicity is on the one side an organic law of memory, dependent upon the revival of transmitted ancestral impressions. A prevailing idea though over-cultivation exhausts its organic correlate, and leads to defective nutrition of that part in the offspring. Hence they do not pursue the same idea as their fathers, but revert to a remoter ancestral historic idea, the organic correlate of which has lain fallow, thus gained strength. It is brought forth as new, receives additions by contiguity and similarity, is ardently pursued, over-cultivated, and in time supplanted by another revival.

But this material side corresponds to an all-important mental one. As an organic process only, the history of periodic ideas is thus satisfactorily explained, but he who holds this explanation to be exhaustive sees but half the problem.

The permanence of a historic idea, I have stated, is in direct proportion to the number of true ideas in its composition; the impression it makes on the organic substrata of memory is in turn in proportion to its permanence. The element of decay is the destructive effects of natural trains of thought out of accord with the logically true trains. These cause defective cerebral nutrition, which is thus seen to arise, so far as influenced by the operations of the memory, from relations of truth and error. There is a physiological tendency in the former to preserve and maintain in activity; in the latter to disappear. The percentage of true concepts which makes up the complexity of a historic idea gives the principal factor towards calculating its probable recurrence. Of course, a second factor is the physiological one of nutrition itself.

The next important distinction in discussing historic ideas is between those which are held consciously, and those which operate unconsciously. The former are always found to be more active, and more amenable to correction. An unconscious idea is a product of the natural, not the logical laws of mind, and is therefore very apt to be largely false. It is always displaced with advantage by a conscious aim.

One of the superficial fallacies of the day, which pass under the name of philosophy, is to maintain that any such historic idea is the best possible one for the time and place in which it is found. I am led to refer to this by the false light it has thrown on religious history. Herbert Spencer remarks in one of his essays:[1] "All religious creeds, during the eras in which they are severally held, are the best that could be held." "All are good for their times and places." So far from this being the case, there never has been a religion but that an improvement in it would have straightway exerted a beneficent effect. Man, no matter what his condition, can always

---

[1] *Essay on the use of Anthropomorphism.* Mr. Spencer's argument, in his own words, is this :—" From the inability under which we labor to conceive of a Deity save as some idealization of ourselves, it inevitably results that in each age, among each people, and to a great extent in each individual, there must arise just that conception of Deity best adapted to the needs of the case." "All are good for their times and places." "All were beneficent in their effects on those who held them." It would be hard to quote from the records of theory-making an example of more complete indifference to acknowledged facts than these quotations set forth.

derive immediate good from higher conceptions of Deity than he himself has elaborated. Nor is the highest conception possible an idealization of self, as I have sufficiently shown in a previous chapter, but is one drawn wholly from the realm of the abstract. Moreover, as a matter of history, we know that in abundant instances, the decay of nations can be traced largely to the base teachings of their religious instructors. To maintain that such religions were "the best possible ones" for the time and place is the absurdest optimism. In what a religion shares of the abstractly true it is beneficent; in what it partakes of the untrue it is deleterious. This, and no other canon, must be our guide.

The ideas of religious history obey the same laws as other historic ideas. They grow, decay, are supplanted and revive again in varying guises, in accordance with the processes of organic nutrition as influenced by the truth or falsity of their component ideas. Their tendency to personification is stronger, because of the much greater nearness they have to the individual desire. The one aspiration of a high-spirited people when subjugated will be freedom; and in the lower stages of culture they will be very certain to fabricate a myth of a deliverer to come.

In like manner, every member of a community shares with his fellow members some wish, hope or ambition dependent on unknown control and therefore religious in character, which will become the "formative idea" of the national religious development.

Of the various ideas in religious history there are three which, through their permanence and frequent revival, we may justly suppose in accordance with the above-mentioned canons to contain a large measure of truth, and yet to be far from wholly true. They may be considered as leading moments in religious growth, yet withal lacking something or other essential to the satisfaction of the religious sentiment. The first of these is the idea of the *perfected individual;* the second the idea of the *perfected commonwealth;* the third, that of *personal survival.* These have been the formative ideas (*Ideen der Gestaltung*) in the prayers, myths, rites and religious institutions of many nations at widely separated times.

Of the two first mentioned it may be said that every extended faith has accepted them to some degree. They are the secret of the alliances of religion with art, with government, with ethics, with science, education and sentiment.

These alliances have often been taken by historians to contain the vital elements of religion itself, and many explanations based on one or another assumption of the kind have been proffered. Religion, while it may embrace any of them, is independent of them all. Its relations to them have been transitory, and the more so as their aims have been local and material. The brief duration of the subjection of religion to such incongenial ties was well compared by Lord Herbert of Cherbury to the early maturity of brutes, who attain their full growth in a year or two, while man needs a quarter of a century.[1] The inferior aims of the religious sentiment were discarded one after another to make way for higher ones, which were slowly dawning upon it. In this progress it was guided largely by the three ideas I have mentioned, which have been in many forms leading stimuli of the religious thought of the race.

First, of the *idea of the perfected individual.*

Many writers have supposed that the contemplation of Power in nature first stirred religious thought in man. Though this is not the view taken in this book, no one will question that the leading trait in the gods of barbarism is physical strength. The naive anthropomorphism of the savage makes his a god of a mighty arm, a giant in stature, puissant and terrible. He hurls the thunderbolt, and piles up the mountains in sport. His name is often The Strong One, as in the Allah, Eloah of the Semitic tongues. Hercules, Chon, Melkarth, Dorsanes, Thor and others were of the most ancient divinities in Greece, Egypt, Phœnicia, India, and Scandinavia, and were all embodiments of physical force. Such, too, was

[1] *De Veritate*, p. 216.

largely the character of the Algonkin Messou, who scooped out the great lakes with his hands and tore up the largest trees by the roots. The huge boulders from the glacial epoch which are scattered over their country are the pebbles he tossed in play or in anger. The cleft in the Andes, through which flows the river Funha, was opened by a single blow of Nemqueteba, chief god of the Muyscas. In all such and a hundred similar legends, easy to quote, we see the notion of strength, brute force, muscular power, was that deemed most appropriate to divinity, and that which he who would be godlike must most sedulously seek. When filled with the god, the votary felt a surpassing vigor. The Berserker fury was found in the wilds of America and Africa, as well as among the Fiords. Sickness and weakness, on the contrary, were signs that the gods were against him. Therefore, in all early stages of culture, the office of priest and physician was one. Conciliation of the gods was the catholicon.

Such deities were fearful to behold. They are represented as mighty of stature and terrible of mien, calculated to appal, not attract, to inspire fear, not to kindle love. In tropical America, in Egypt, in Thibet, almost where you will, there is little to please the eye in the pictures and statues of deities.

In Greece alone, a national temperament, marvellously sensitive to symmetry, developed the combination of maximum strength with perfect form in the sun-god, Apollo, and of grace with beauty in Aphrodite. The Greeks were the apostles of the religion of beauty. Their philosophic thought saw the permanent in the Form, which outlives strength, and is that alone in which the race has being. In its transmission love is the agent, and Aphrodite, unmatched in beauty and mother of love, was a creation worthy of their devotion. Thus with them the religious sentiment still sought its satisfaction in the individual, not indeed in the muscle, but in the feature and expression.

When the old gods fell, the Christian fathers taught their flocks to abhor the beautiful as one with the sensual. St. Clement of Alexandria and Tertullian describe Christ as ugly of visage and undersized, a sort of Socrates in appearance.[1] Christian art was long in getting recognition. The heathens were the first to represent in picture and statues Christ and the apostles, and for long the fathers of the church opposed the multiplication of such images, saying that the inward beauty was alone desirable. Christian art reached its highest inspiration under the influence of Greek culture after the fall of Constantinople.

---

[1] August Neander, *Geschichte der Christlichen Religion und Kirche*, Bd. i., ss. 160, 346. (Gotha, 1856.) St. Clement's description of Christ is Τον οψιν αισχρον. Tertullian says : " Nec humanæ honestatis corpus fuit, nedum celestis claritatis."

In the very year, however, that Rafaello Sanzio met his premature death, Luther burned the decretals of the pope in the market-place of Wittenberg, and preached a doctrine as hostile to art as was that of Eusebius and Chrysostom. There was no longer any hope for the religion of beauty.

Nevertheless, under the influence of the revival of ancient art which arose with Winckelmann towards the close of the last century, a gospel of esthetics was preached. Its apostles were chiefly Germans, and among them Schiller and Goethe are not inconspicuous names. The latter, before his long life was closed, began to see the emptiness of such teachings, and the violence perpetrated on the mind by forcing on the religious sentiment the food fit only for the esthetic emotions.

The highest conception of individual perfection is reached in a character whose physical and mental powers are symmetrically trained, and always directed by conscious reason to their appropriate ends. Self-government, founded on self-knowledge, wards off the pangs of disappointment by limiting ambition to the attainable. The affections and emotions, and the pleasures of sensation as well, are indulged in or abstained from, but never to the darkening of the intellect. All the talents are placed at usury; every power exercised systematically and fruitfully with a consecration to a noble purpose.

This is the religion of culture. None other ranks among its adherents so many great minds; men, as Carlyle expresses it, of much religiosity, if of little religion. The ideal is a taking one. Such utter self-reliance, not from ignorance, but from the perfection of knowledge, was that which Buddha held up to his followers: "Self is the God of self; who else should be the God?" In this century Goethe, Wordsworth, beyond all others Wilhelm von Humboldt, have set forth this ideal. Less strongly intellectual natures, as Maine de Biran, De Senancourt, and Matthew Arnold, listen with admiration, but feel how unknown to the mass of human kind must remain the tongue these masters speak.

Thus did the religious sentiment seek its satisfaction in the idealization, first of physical force, then of form, and last of mental force, but in each case turned away unsatisfied. Wherein did these ideals fail? The first mentioned in exalting power over principle, might over right. As was well said by the philosophical Novalis: "The ideal of morality has no more dangerous rival than the ideal of physical strength, of the most vigorous life. Through it man is transformed into a reasoning beast, whose brutal cleverness has a fascination for weak minds."[1] The religion of beauty failed in that it addressed

[1] Novalis, *Schriften*, B. i., s. 244.

the esthetic emotions, not the reasoning power. Art does not promote the good; it owes no fealty to either utility or ethics: in itself, it must be, in the negative sense of the words, at once useless and immoral. "Nature is not its standard, nor is truth its chief end."[1] Its spirit is repose, "the perfect form in perfect rest;" whereas the spirit of religion is action because of imperfection. Even the gods must know of suffering, and partake, in incarnations, of the miseries of men.

In the religion of culture what can we blame? That it is lacking in the impulses of action through the isolation it fosters; that it is and must be limited to a few, for it provides no defense for the weaknesses the many inherit; that its tendency is antagonistic to religion, as it cuts away the feeling of dependence, and the trust in the unknown; that it allows too little to enthusiasm ever to become a power.

On the other hand, what momenta of true religious thought have these ideals embraced? Each presents some. Physical vigor, regarded as a sign of complete nutrition, is an indispensable preliminary to the highest religion. Correct thought cannot be, without sufficient and appropriate food. If the nourishment is inadequate, defective energy of the brain will be transmitted, and the offspring will revert ancestrally to a lower plane of thought. "It thus happens that

---

[1] A. Bain, *The Senses and the Intellect*, p. 607.

the minds of persons of high religious culture by ancestral descent, and the intermarriage of religious families, so strangely end in the production of children totally devoid of moral sense and religious sentiment—moral imbeciles in short."[1] From such considerations of the necessity of physical vigor to elevated thought, Descartes predicted that if the human race ever attain perfection it will be chiefly through the art of medicine. Not alone from emotions of sympathy did the eminent religious teachers of past ages maintain that the alleviation and prevention of suffering is the first practical duty of man; but it was from a perhaps unconscious perception of the antagonism of bodily degeneration to mental progress.

So, too, the religion of beauty and art contains an indefeasible germ of true religious thought. Art sees the universal in the isolated fact; it redeemed the coarse symbol of earlier days by associating it with the emotions of joy, instead of fear; commencing with an exaltation of the love to sex, it etherealized and ennobled passion; it taught man to look elsewhere than to material things for his highest pleasure, for the work of art always has its fortune in the imagination and not in the senses of the observer; conceptions of order and harmony are

[1] Dr. T. Laycock, *On some Organic Laws of Memory*, in the *Journal of Mental Science*, July, 1875, p. 178.

familiar to it; its best efforts seek to bring all the affairs of life under unity and system;[1] and thus it strengthens the sentiment of moral government, which is the first postulate of religion.

The symmetry of the individual, as understood in the religion of culture, is likewise a cherished article of true religion. Thus only can it protect personality against the pitfalls of self-negation and absorption, which communism and pantheism dig for it. The integrity and permanence of the person is the keystone to religion, as it is to philosophy and ethics. None but a false teacher would measure our duty to our neighbor by a higher standard than our love to ourselves. The love of God alone is worthy to obscure it.

Professor Steinthal has said: "Every people has its own religion. The national temperament hears the tidings and interprets them as it can."[2] On the other hand, Humboldt—perhaps

---

[1] Speaking of the mission of the artist, Wilhelm von Humboldt says: "Die ganze Natur, treu und vollständig beobachtet, mit sich hinüber zu tragen, d. h. den Stoff seiner Erfahrungen dem Umfange der Welt gleich zu machen, diese ungeheure Masse einzelner und abgerissener Erscheinungen in eine l'ungetrennte Einheit und ein organisirtes Ganzes zu verwandeln; und dies durch alle die Organe zu thun, die ihm hierzu verliehen sind,—ist das letzte Ziel seines intellectuellen Bemühen." *Ueber Goethe's Hermann und Dorothea*, Ab. IV.

[2] *Zeitschrift für Völkerpsychologie*, B. I. s. 48.

the profoundest thinker on these subjects of his generation—doubted whether religions can be measured in reference to nations and sects, because "religion is altogether subjective, and rests solely on the conceptive powers of the individual."[1] Whatever the creed, a pure mind will attach itself to its better elements, a base one to its brutal and narrow doctrines. A national religion can only be regarded as an average, applicable to the majority, not entirely correct of the belief of any one individual, wholly incorrect as to a few. Yet it is indubitable that the national temperament creates the ideal which gives the essence of religion. Races like the Tartar Mongols, who, as we are informed by the Abbé Huc, not unfrequently move their tents several times a day, out of simple restlessness, cannot desire the same stability that is sought by other races, who have the beaver's instinct for building and colonizing, such as the Romans. Buddhism, which sets up the ideal of the individual, is an acceptable theory to the former, while the latter, from earliest ages, fostered religious views which taught the subordination of the individual to the community, in other words, the *idea of the perfected commonwealth*.

This is the conception at the base of all

---

[1] *Gesammelte Werke.* Bd. VII., s. 63.

theocracies, forms of government whose statutes are identified with the precepts of religion. Instead of a constitution there is the Law, given and sanctioned by God as a rule of action.

The Law is at first the Myth applied. Its object is as much to propitiate the gods as to preserve social order. It is absolute because it is inspired. Many of its ordinances as drawn from the myth are inapplicable to man, and are unjust or frivolous. Yet such as it is, it rules the conduct of the commonwealth and expresses the ideal of its perfected condition.

All the oldest codes of laws are religious, and are alleged revelations. The Pentateuch, the Avesta, the Laws of Manu, the Twelve Tables, the Laws of Seleucus, all carry the endorsement, "And God said." Their real intention is to teach the relation of man to God, rather than the relations of man to man. On practical points—on the rights of property, on succession and wills, on contracts, on the adoption of neighbors, and on the treatment of enemies—they often violate the plainest dictates of natural justice, of common humanity, even of family affection. Their precepts are frequently frivolous, sometimes grossly immoral. But if these laws are compared with the earliest myths and cults, and the opinions then entertained of the gods, and how to propitiate them, it becomes easy to see how the precepts of the law flowed from these inchoate imaginings of the religious sentiment.[1]

The improvement of civil statutes did not come through religion. Experience, observation and free thought taught man justice, and his kindlier emotions were educated by the desire to cherish and preserve which arose from family and social ties. As these came to be recognized as necessary relations of society, religion appropriated them, incorporated them into her ideal, and even claimed them as her revelations. History largely invalidates this claim. The moral progress of mankind has been mainly apart from dogmatic teachings, often in conflict with them. An established rule of faith may enforce obedience to its statutes, but can never develop morals. "True virtue is independent of every religion, and incompatible with any which is accepted on authority."[2]

Yet thinkers, even the best of them, appear to have had difficulty in discerning any nobler arena for the religious sentiment than the social one. "Religion," says Matthew Arnold, "is conduct." It is the power "which makes for righteousness." "As civil law," said Voltaire, "enforces morality in public, so the use of religion is to compel it in private life." "A complete

---

[1] See this forcibly brought out and abundantly illustrated in the work of M. Coulange, *La Cité Antique*.

[2] W. von Humboldt, *Gesammelte Werke*. Bd. VII., p. 72.

morality," observes a contemporary Christian writer, "meets all the practical ends of religion."[1] In such expressions man's social relations, his duty to his neighbor, are taken to exhaust religion. It is still the idea of the commonwealth, the religion of morality, the submission to a law recognized as divine. Whether the law is a code of ethics, the decision of a general council, or the ten commandments, it is alike held to be written by the finger of God, and imperative. Good works are the demands of such religion.

Catholicism, which is altogether theocratic and authoritative, which pictures the church as an ideal commonwealth, has always most flourished in those countries where the Roman colonies left their more important traces. The reformation of Protestantism was a reversion to the ideal of the individual, which was that of ancient Teutonic faith. In more recent times Catholicism itself has modified the rigidity of its teachings in favor of the religion of sentiment, as it has been called, inaugurated by Chateaubriand, and which is that attractive form seen in the writings of Madame Swetchine and the La Ferronnais. These elevated souls throw a charm around the immolation of self, which the egotism of the Protestant rarely matches.

---

[1] II. L. Liddon, Canon of St. Paul's. *Some Elements of Religion*, p. 84.

Thus the ideal of the commonwealth is found in those creeds which give prominence to law, to ethics, and to sentiment, the altruistic elements of mind. It fails, because its authority is antagonistic to morality in that it impedes the search for the true. Neither is morality religion, for it deals with the relative, while religion should guide itself by the absolute. Every great religious teacher has violated the morality of his day. Even sentiment, attractive as it is, is no ground on which to build a church. It is, at best, one of the lower emotional planes of action. Love itself, which must be the kernel of every true religion, is not in earthly relations an altruistic sentiment. The measure and the source of all such love, is self-love. The creed which rejects this as its corner stone will build in vain.

While, therefore, the advantages of organization and action are on the side of the faiths which see in religion a form of government, they present fewer momenta of religious thought than those which encourage the greater individuality. All forms and reforms, remarks Machiavelli, in one of his notes to Livy, have been brought about by the exertions of one man.[1] Religious

---

[1] The Chevalier Bunsen completed the moral estimate of the one-man-power, thus acknowledged by Machiavelli, in these words: "Alles Grosse geht aus vom Einzelnen, aber nur in dem Masse, als dieser das Ich dem Ganzen opfert." *Gott in der Geschichte*, Bd. I., s. 38.

reforms, especially, never have originated in majorities. The reformatory decrees of the Council of Trent are due to Martin Luther.

Either ideal, raised to its maximum, not only fails to satisfy the religious sentiment, but puts upon it a forced meaning, and is therefore not what this sentiment asks. This may be illustrated by comparing two remarkable works, which, by a singular coincidence, were published in the same year, and which better than any others present these ideals pushed to their extreme. It is characteristic of them that neither professes to treat of religion, but of politics. The one is entitled, "*An Attempt to define the limits of Government*," and is by Wilhelm von Humboldt; the other is the better known work of Auguste Comte, his "*System of Positive Polity*."[1]

The first lays down the principle that the highest end of man is the utmost symmetrical education of his own powers in their individual peculiarities. To accomplish this, he must enjoy the largest freedom of thought and action consistent with the recognition of the same right in others. In regard to religion, the state should have nothing to do with aiding it, but should

---

[1] W. von Humboldt, *Ideen zu einem Versuch, die Gränzen der Wirksamkeit des Staats zu bestimmen*, Breslau, 1851. Auguste Comte, *Système de Politique Positive*, Paris, 1851-4. The former was written many years before its publication.

protect the individual in his opposition to any authoritative form of it. As a wholly personal and subjective matter, social relations do not concern it. In fine, the aim of both government and education should be the development of an individualism in which an enlightened intellect controls and directs all the powers toward an exalted self-cultivation.

Comte reverses this picture. His fundamental principle is to subordinate the sum total of our existence to our social relations; real life is to live in others; not the individual but humanity is the only worthy object of effort. Social polity therefore includes the whole of development; the intellect should have no other end but to subserve the needs of the race, and always be second to the altruistic sentiments. Love toward others should absorb self-love. "*Il est encore meilleur d'aimer que d'être aimé.*"

Such is the contrast between the ideal of the individual as exhibited by the Religion of Culture, and the ideal of the commonwealth as portrayed in the Religion of Humanity.

The whole duty of man, says the one school, is to live for others; nay, says the other, it is to live intelligently for himself; the intellect, says the former, should always be subordinated to society, and be led by the emotions; intellect, says the latter, should ever be in the ascendant, and absolutely control and direct the emotions; the theoretical object of government, says the former, is to enable the affections and thoughts to pass into action; not so, says the latter, its only use is to give the individual secure leisure to develope his own affections and thoughts. Mutual relation is the key note of the former, independence of the latter; the former is the apotheosis of love, the latter of reason.

Strictly and literally the apotheosis. For, differing as they do on such vital points, they both agree in dispensing with the ideas of God and immortality as conceptions superfluous in the realization of the theoretical perfection they contemplate. Not that either scheme omits the religious sentiment. On the contrary, it is especially prominent in one, and very well marked in the other. Both assume its growing prominence, never its extinction. Both speak of it as an integral part of man's highest nature.

Comte and Humboldt were thinkers too profound to be caught by the facile fallacy that the rapid changes in religious thought betoken the early abrogation of all creeds. Lessing, the philosophers of the French revolution, James Mill, Schopenhauer and others fell into this error. They were not wiser than the clown of Horace, who seated himself by the rushing stream, thinking it must soon run itself out—

> Expectat rusticus dum defluat amnis; at ille
> Labitur et labetur in omne volubilis ævum.

Vain is the dream that man will ever reach the point when he will think no more of the gods. Dogmas may disappear, but religion will flourish; destroy the temple and sow it with salt, in a few days it rises again built for aye on the solid ground of man's nature.

. So long as the race is upon earth, just so long will the religious sentiment continue to crave its appropriate food, and this at last is recognized even by those who estimate it at the lowest. "To yield this sentiment reasonable satisfaction," observes Professor Tyndall in one of his best known addresses, "is the problem of problems at the present hour. It is vain to oppose it with a view to its extirpation." The "general thaw of theological creeds," which Spencer remarks upon, is no sign of the loss of interest in religious subjects, but the reverse. Coldness and languor are the premonitions of death, not strife and defence.

But as the two moments of religious thought which I have now discussed have both reached their culmination in a substantial repudiation of religion, that which stimulates the religious sentiment to-day must be something different from either. This I take to be the *idea of personal survival* after physical death, or, as it is generally called, the doctrine of the immortality of the soul.

This is the main dogma in the leading religions of the world to-day. "A God," remarks

Sir William Hamilton, speaking for the enlightened Christians of his generation, " is to us of practical interest, only inasmuch as he is the condition of our immortality." [1] In his attractive work, *La Vie Eternelle*, whose large popularity shows it to express the prevailing views of modern Protestant thought, Ernest Naville takes pains to distinguish that Christianity is not a means of living a holy life so much as one of gaining a blessed hereafter. The promises of a life after death are numerous and distinct in the New Testament. Most of the recommendations of action and suffering in this world are based on the doctrine of compensation in the world to come.

Mohammed taught the same tenet with equal or even greater emphasis. In one sura he says: " To whatever is evil may they be likened who believe not in a future life ; " and elsewhere : " As for the blessed ones—their place is Paradise. There shall they dwell so long as the heavens and the earth endure, enjoying the imperishable bounties of God. But as for those who shall be consigned to misery, their place is the Fire. There shall they abide so long as the heavens and the earth shall last, unless God wills it otherwise." [2]

In Buddhism, as generally understood, the

---

[1] *Lectures on Metaphysics*, Vol. I., p. 23.

[2] *The Koran*, Suras xi., xvi.

doctrine of a future life is just as clear. Not only does the soul wander from one to another animal body, but when it has completed its peregrinations and reaches its final abode, it revels in all sorts of bliss. For the condition of Nirvana, understood by philosophical Buddhists as that of the extinction of desires even to the desire of life, and of the complete enlightenment of the mind even to the recognition that existence itself is an illusion, has no such meaning to the millions who profess themselves the followers of the sage of Kapilavastu. They take it to be a material Paradise with pleasures as real as those painted by Mohammed, wherein they will dwell beyond all time, a reward for their devotions and faith in this life.

These three religions embrace three-fourths of the human race and all its civilized nations, with trifling exceptions. They displaced and extinguished the older creeds and in a few centuries controlled the earth; but as against each other their strife has been of little avail. The reason is, they share the same momentum of religious thought, differing in its interpretation not more among themselves than do orthodox members of either faith in their own fold. Many enlightened Muslims and Christians, for example, consider the descriptions of Paradise given in the Koran and the Apocalypse to convey wholly spiritual meanings.

There has been so much to surprise in the rapid extension of these faiths that the votaries of each claim manifest miraculous interposition. The religious idea of an after life is a sufficient moment to account for the phenomenon. I say the *religious* idea, for, with one or two exceptions, however distinct had been the belief in a hereafter, that belief had not a religious coloring until they gave it such. This distinction is an important one.

Students of religions have hitherto attributed too much weight to the primitive notion of an existence after death. It is common enough, but it rarely has anything at all to do with the simpler manifestations of the religious sentiment. These are directed to the immediate desires of the individual or the community, and do not look beyond the present life. The doctrine of compensation hereafter is foreign to them. I have shown this at length so far as the religions of America were concerned. "Neither the delights of a heaven on the one hand, nor the terrors of a hell on the other were ever held out by priests or sages as an incentive to well doing, or a warning to the evil disposed."[1] The same is true of the classical religions of Greece and Rome, of Carthage and Assyria. Even in Egypt the manner of death and the rites of interment had much more to do with the fate of the soul,

[1] *The Myths of the New World*, Chap. IX.

than had its thoughts and deeds in the flesh. The opinions of Socrates and Plato on the soul as something which always existed and whose after life is affected by its experiences here, struck the Athenians as novel and innovating.

On the other hand, the ancient Germans had a most lively faith in the life hereafter. Money was loaned in this world to be repaid in the next. But with them also, as with the Aztecs, the future was dependent on the character or mode of death rather than the conduct of life. He who died the "straw-death" on the couch of sickness looked for little joy in the hereafter; but he who met the "spear-death" on the field of battle went at once to Odin, to the hall of Valhalla, where the heroes of all time assembled to fight, eat boar's fat and drink beer. Even this rude belief gave them such an ascendancy over the materialistic Romans, that these distinctly felt that in the long run they must succumb to a bravery which rested on such a mighty moment as this.[1]

The Israelites do not seem to have entertained any general opinion on an existence after death. No promise in the Old Testament refers to a future life. The religion there taught nowhere

---

[1] Jacob Grimm quite overlooked this important element in the religion of the ancient Germans. It is ably set forth by Adolf Holtzmann, *Deutsche Mythologie*, s. 196 sqq. (Leipzig, 1874).

looks beyond the grave. It is materialistic to the fullest extent. Hence, a large body of orthodox Jewish philosophers, the Sadducees, denied the existence of the soul apart from the body.

The central doctrine of the teachings of Jesus of Nazareth, the leading impulse which he gave to the religious thought of his age, was that the thinking part of man survives his physical death, and that its condition does not depend on the rites of interment, as other religions then taught,[1] but on the character of its thoughts during life here. Filled with this new and sublime idea, he developed it in its numerous applications, and drew from it those startling inferences, which, to this day, stagger his followers, and have been in turn, the terror and derision of his foes. This he saw, that against a mind

---

[1] The seemingly heartless reply he made to one of his disciples, who asked permission to perform the funeral rites at his father's grave: "Follow me; and let the dead bury their dead," is an obvious condemnation of one of the most widespread superstitions of the ancient world. So, according to an ingenious suggestion of Lord Herbert of Cherbury, was the fifth commandment of Moses: "Ne parentum seriem tanquam primam aliquam causam suspicerent homines, et proinde cultum aliquem Divinum illis deferrent, qualem ex honore parentum sperare liceat benedictionem, docuit." *De Veritate*, p. 231.

Herbert Spencer in his *Essay on the Origin of Animal Worship*, calls ancestral worship "the universal first form of religious belief." This is very far from correct, but it is easy to see how a hasty thinker would be led into the error by the prominence of the ancient funereal ceremonies.

inwardly penetrated with the full conviction of a life hereafter, obtainable under known conditions, the powers of this world are utterly futile, and its pleasures hollow phantoms.

The practical energy of this doctrine was immensely strengthened by another, which is found very obscurely, if at all, stated in his own words, but which was made the central point of their teaching by his immediate followers. The Christianity they preached was not a philosophical scheme for improving the race, but rested on the historical fact of a transaction between God and man, and while they conceded everlasting existence to all men, all would pass it in the utmost conceivable misery, except those who had learned of these historical events, and understood them as the church prescribed.

As the ancient world placed truth in ideas and not in facts, no teaching could well have been more radically contrary to its modes of thought; and the doctrine once accepted, the spirit of proselytizing came with it.

I have called this idea a new one to the first century of our era, and so it was in Europe and Syria. But in India, Sakyamuni, probably five hundred years before, had laid down in sententious maxims the philosophical principle which underlies the higher religious doctrine of a future life. These are his words, and if through the efforts of reasoning we ever reach a demonstration of the immortality of the soul, we shall do it by pursuing the argument here indicated: "Right thought is the path to life everlasting. Those who think do not die."[1]

Truth alone contains the elements of indefinite continuity; and truth is found only in the idea, in correct thought.

Error in the intellectual processes corresponds to pain in sensation; it is the premonition of waning life, of threatened annihilation; it contains the seed of cessation of action or death. False reasoning is self-destructive. The man who believes himself invulnerable will scarcely survive his first combat. A man's true ideas are the most he can hope, and all that he should wish, to carry with him to a life hereafter. Falsehood, sin, is the efficient agent of death. As Bishop Hall says: "There is a kind of not-being in sin; for sin is not an existence of somewhat that is, but a deficiency of that rectitude which should be; it is a privation, as blindness is a privation of sight."

While the religious doctrine of personal survival has thus a position defensible on grounds of reason as being that of the inherent permanence of self-conscious truth, it also calls to its aid and indefinitely elevates the most powerful of all the emotions, *love*. This, as I have shown

[1] Dhammapada, 21.

in the second chapter, is the sentiment which is characteristic of *preservative* acts. Self-love, which is prominent in the idea of the perfected individual, sex-love, which is the spirit of the multiform religious symbolism of the reproductive act, and the love of race, which is the chief motor in the religion of humanity, are purified of their grosser demands and assigned each its meet post in the labor of uniting the conceptions of the true under the relation of personality.

The highest development of which such love is capable arises through the contemplation of those verities which are abstract and eternal, and which thus set forth, to the extent the individual mind is capable of receiving it, the completed notion of diuturnity. This highest love is the "love of God." A Supreme Intelligence, one to which all truth is perfect, must forever dwell in such contemplation. Therefore the deeper minds of Christianity define man's love of God, as God's love to himself. "Eternal life," says Ernest Naville, "is in its principle the union with God and the joy that results from that union."[1] The pious William Law wrote: "No man can reach God with his love, or have union with Him by it, but he who is inspired with that one same spirit of love, with

[1] *La Vie Eternelle*, p. 339.

which God loved himself from all eternity, before there was any creation."[1]

Attractive as the idea of personal survival is in itself, and potent as it has been as a moment of religious thought, it must be ranked among those that are past. While the immortality of the soul retains its interest as a speculative inquiry, I venture to believe that as an idea in religious history, it is nigh inoperative; that as an element in devotional life it is of not much weight; and that it will gradually become less so, as the real meaning of religion reaches clearer interpretations.

Its decay has been progressive, and common to all the creeds which taught it as a cardinal doctrine, though most marked in Christianity. A century ago Gibbon wrote: " The ancient Christians were animated by a contempt for their present existence, and by a just confidence of immortality, of which the doubtful but imperfect faith of modern ages cannot give us any adequate notion."[2] How true this is can be appreciated only by those who study this doctrine in the lives and writings of the martyrs and fathers of the primitive church.

The breach which Gibbon remarked has been indefinitely widened since his time. What has

[1] *The Decline and Fall of the Roman Empire*, Vol. I., ch. XV.
[2] *Address to the Clergy*, p. 16.

brought this about, and what new moment in religious thought seems about to supply its place, will form an appropriate close to the present series of studies. In its examination, I shall speak only of Christian thought, since it leads the way which other systems will ultimately follow.

In depicting the influences which have led and are daily leading with augmented force to the devitalizing of the doctrine of immortality, I may with propriety confine myself to those which are themselves strictly religious. For the change I refer to is not one brought about by the opponents of religion, by materialistic doctrines, but is owing to the development of the religious sentiment itself. Instead of tending to an abrogation of that sentiment, it may be expected to ennoble its emotional manifestations and elevate its intellectual conceptions.

Some of these influences are historical, as the repeated disappointments in the second coming of Christ, and the interest of proselytizing churches to interpret this event allegorically. Those which I deem of more importance, however, are such as are efficient to-day, and probably will continue to be the main agents in the immediate future of religious development. They are:

(1.) The recognition of the grounds of ethics.

(2.) The recognition of the cosmical relations.

(3.) The clearer defining of life.

(4.) The growing immateriality of religious thought.

(1.) The authority of the Law was assumed in the course of time by most Christian churches, and the interests of morality and religion were claimed to be identical. The Roman church with its developed casuistry is ready to prescribe the proper course of conduct in every emergency; and if we turn to many theological writers of other churches, Dick's *Philosophy of Religion* for instance, we find moral conduct regarded as the important aim of the Christian life. Morality without religion, works without faith, are pronounced to be of no avail in a religious, and of very questionable value in a social sense. Some go so far as to deny that a person indifferent to the prevailing tenets of religion can lead a pure and moral life. Do away with the belief in a hereafter of rewards and punishments, say these, and there is nothing left to restrain men from the worst excesses, or at least from private sin.

Now, however, the world is growing to perceive that morality is separable from religion; that it arose independently, from a gradual study of the relations of man to man, from principles of equity inherent in the laws of thought, and from considerations of expediency which deprive its precepts of the character of universality.

Religion is subjective, and that in which it exerts an influence on morality is not its contents, but the reception of them peculiar to the individual. Experience alone has taught man morals; pain and pleasure are the forms of its admonitions; and each generation sees more clearly that the principles of ethics are based on immutable physical laws. Moreover, it has been shown to be dangerous to rest morality on the doctrine of a future life; for apart from the small effect the terrors of a hereafter have on many sinners, as that doctrine is frequently rejected, social interests suffer. And, finally, it is debasing and hurtful to religion to make it a substitute for police magistracy.[1]

The highest religion would certainly enforce the purest morality; but it is equally true that such a religion would enjoin much not approved by the current opinions of the day. The spirit of the reform inaugurated by Luther was a protest against the subjection of the religious sentiment to a moral code. With the independence thus achieved, it came to be recognized that to the full extent that morality is essential to religion, it can be reached as well or better without a system of rewards and punishments after death,

---

[1] "Toute religion, qu'on se permet de défendre comme une croyance qu'il est utile de laisser au peuple, ne peut plus espérer qu'une agonie plus ou moins prolongée." Condorcet, *De l'Esprit Humain*, Ep. V.

than with one. Both religion and morality stand higher, when a conception of an after life for this purpose is dropped.

(2.) The recognition of the cosmical relations has also modified the views of personal survival. The expansion of the notions of space and time by the sciences of geology and astronomy has, as I before remarked, done away with the ancient belief that the culminating catastrophe of the universe will be the destruction of this world. An insignificant satellite of a third rate sun, which, with the far grander suns whose light we dimly discern at night, may all be swept away in some flurry of "cosmical weather," that the formation or the dissolution of such a body would be an event of any beyond the most insignificant importance, is now known to be almost ridiculous. To assert that at the end of a few or a few thousand years, on account of events transpiring on the surface of this planet, the whole relationship of the universe will be altered, a new heaven and a new earth be formed, and all therein be made subservient to the joys of man, becomes an indication of an arrogance which deserves to be called a symptom of insanity. Thus, much of the teleology both of the individual and the race taught by the primitive and medieval church undergoes serious alterations. The literal meaning of the millennium, the New Jerusalem, and the reign of God on earth has been practically discarded.

With the disappearance of the ancient opinion that the universe was created for man, the sun to light him by day and the stars by night, disappeared also the later thesis that the happiness or the education of man was the aim of the Order in Things. The extent and duration of matter, if they indicate any purpose at all, suggest one incomparably vaster than this; while the laws of mind, which alone distinctly point to purpose, reveal one in which pain and pleasure have no part or lot, and one in which man has so small a share that it seems as if it must be indifferent what his fate may be. The slightest change in the atmosphere of the globe will sweep away his species forever.

Schopenhauer classified all religions as optimisms or pessimisms. The faith of the future will be neither. What is agreeable or disagreeable to man will not be its standard of the excellence of the universe. However unwillingly, he is at last brought to confess that his comfort is not the chief nor even any visible aim of the order in things. In the course of that order it may be, nay, it is nigh certain, that the human species will pass through decadence to extinction along with so many other organisms. Neither as individuals nor as a race, neither in regard to this life nor to the next, does the idea of God, when ennobled by a contemplation of the cosmical relations, permit to man the effrontery of claiming that this universe and all that therein is was made with an eye to his wants and wishes, whether to gratify or to defeat them.

(3.) The closer defining of life as a result of physical force, and the recognition of mind as a connotation of organism, promise to be active in elevating religious conceptions, but at the expense of the current notions of personality. Sensation and voluntary motion are common to the fetus, the brute and the plant, as well as to man. They are not part of his "soul." Intellect and consciousness, as I have shown, exclude sensation, and in these, if anywhere, he must look for his immortal part. Even here, error works destruction, and ignorance plants no seed of life. We are driven back to the teaching of Buddha, that true thought alone is that which does not die.

Why should we ask more? What else is worth saving? Our present personality is a train of ideas base and noble, true and false, coherent through the contiguity of organs nourished from a common center. Another personality is possible, one of true ideas coherent through conscious similarity, independent of sensation, as dealing with topics not commensurate with it. Yet were this refuge gained, it leaves not much of the dogma that every man has an indestructible conscious soul, which will endure always, no matter what his conduct or thoughts have been. Rather does it favor the opinion expressed so well by Matthew Arnold in one of his sonnets :

> " He who flagged not in the earthly strife
> From strength to strength advancing—only he,
> His soul well knit and all his battles won,
> Mounts, and that hardly, to eternal life."

Not only has the received doctrine of a " soul," as an undying something different from mind and peculiar to man, received no support from a closer study of nature,— rather objections amounting to refutation,— but it has reacted injuriously on morals, and through them on religion itself. Buddha taught that the same spark of immortality exists in man and brute, and actuated by this belief laid down the merciful rule to his disciples: "Do harm to no breathing thing." The apostle Paul on the other hand, recognizing in the lower animals no such claim on our sympathy, asks with scorn: " Doth God care for oxen?" and actually strips from a humane provision of the old Mosaic code its spirit of charity, in order to make it subserve a point in his polemic.

(4.) As the arrogance of the race has thus met a rebuke, so has the egotism of the individual. His religion at first was a means of securing material benefits ; then a way to a joyous existence beyond the tomb : the love of self all the time in the ascendant.

This egoism in the doctrine of personal survival has been repeatedly flung at it by satirists, and commented on by philosophers. The Christian who "hopes to be saved by grossly believing" has been felt on all hands to be as mean in his hope, as he is contemptible in his way of attaining it. To center all our religious efforts to the one end of getting joy—however we may define it—for our individual selves, has something repulsive in it to a deeply religious mind. Yet that such in the real significance of the doctrine of personal survival is granted by its ablest defenders. "The general expectation of future happiness can afford satisfaction only as it is a present object to the principle of self-love," says Dr. Butler, the eminent Lord Bishop of Durham, than whom no acuter analyst has written on the religious nature of man.

Yet nothing is more certain than that the spirit of true religion wages constant war with the predominance or even presence of selfish aims. Self-love is the first and rudest form of the instinct of preservation. It is sublimed and sacrificed on the altar of holy passion. "Self," exclaims the fervid William Law, "is both atheist and idolater; atheist, because it rejects God; idolater, because it is its own idol." Even when this lowest expression of the preservative instinct rises but to the height of sex-love, it renounces self, and rejoices in martyrdom. "All for love, or the world well lost," has been the motto of too many tragedies to be doubted now. By the side of the ancient Roman or the soldier of the French revolution, who through mere love of country marched joyously to certain death from which he expected no waking, does not the martyr compare unfavorably, who meets the same death, but does so because he believes that thereby he secures endless and joyous life? Is his love as real, as noble, as unselfish?

Even the resistless physical energy which the clear faith in the life hereafter has so often imparted, becomes something uncongenial to the ripened religious meditation. Such faith brings about mighty effects in the arena of man's struggles, but it does so through a sort of mechanical action. An ulterior purpose is ahead. to wit, the salvation of the soul, and it may be regarded as one of the best established principles of human effort that every business is better done, when it is done for its own sake, out of liking for it, than for results expected from it.

Of nothing is this more just than religion. Those blossoms of spiritual perfection, the purified reason, the submissive will, the sanctifying grace of abstract ideas, find no propitious airs amid the violent toil for personal survival, whether that is to be among the mead jugs of Valhalla, the dark-eyed houris of Paradise, or the "solemn troops and sweet society" of Christian dreams. Unmindful of these, the saintly psyche looks to nothing beyond truth; it asks no definite, still less personal, end to which this truth is to be applied; to find it is to love it, and to love it is enough.

The doctrine I here broach, is no strange one to Christian thought. To be sure the exhortation, "Save your soul from Hell," was almost the sole incentive to religion in the middle ages, and is still the burden of most sermons. But St. Paul was quickened with a holier fire, that consumed and swept away such a personal motive, when he wrote: "Yea, I could wish that I myself were cast out from Christ as accursed, for the sake of my brethren, my kinsmen according to the flesh."[1] St. Augustine reveals the touch of the same inspiration in his passionate exclamation: "Far, O Lord, far from the heart of thy servant be it that I should rejoice in any joy whatever. The blessed life is the joy in truth alone."[2] And amid the pæans to everlasting life which fill the pages of the *De Imitatione Christi*, the medieval monk saw something yet greater, when he puts in the mouth of God the Father, the warning: "The wise lover thinks not of the gift, but of the love of the

---

[1] *Romans*, ch. ix., v. 3.
[2] "Beata quippe vita est gaudium de veritate." Augustini *Confessionum*, Lib. x., caps. xxii., xxiii.

giver. He rests not in the reward, but in Me, beyond all rewards."[1] The mystery of great godliness is, that he who has it is as one who seeking nothing yet finds all things, who asking naught for his own sake, neither in the life here nor yet hereafter, gains that alone which is of worth in either.

Pressed by such considerations, the pious Schleiermacher threw down the glaive on the side of religion half a century ago when he wrote : "Life to come, as popularly conceived, is the last enemy which speculative criticism has to encounter, and, if possible, to overcome." The course he marked out, however, was not that which promises success. Recurring to the austere theses of Spinoza, he sought to bring them into accord with a religion of emotion. The result was a refined Pantheism with its usual deceptive solutions.

What recourse is left? Where are we to look for the intellectual moment of religion in the future? Let us review the situation.

The religious sentiment has been shown to be the expression of unfulfilled desire, but this desire peculiar as dependent on unknown power. Material advantages do not gratify it, nor even

---

[1] "Prudens amator non tam donum amantis considerat, quam dantis amorem. Nobilis amator non quiescit in dono, sed in me super omne donum." *De Imitatione Christi*, Lib. iii., cap. vi.

spiritual joy when regarded as a personal sentiment. Preservation by and through relation with absolute intelligence has appeared to be the meaning of that "love of God" which alone yields it satisfaction. Even this is severed from its received doctrinal sense by the recognition of the speculative as above the numerical unity of that intelligence, and the limitation of personality which spiritual thought demands. The eternal laws of mind guarantee perpetuity to the extent they are obeyed—and no farther. They differ from the laws of force in that they convey a message which cannot be doubted concerning the purport of the order in nature, which is itself "the will of God." That message in its application is the same which with more or less articulate utterance every religion speaks—Seek truth: do good. Faith in that message, confidence in and willing submission to that order, this is all the religious sentiment needs to bring forth its sweetest flowers, its richest fruits.

Such is the ample and satisfying ground which remains for the religion of the future to build upon. It is a result long foreseen by the clearer minds of Christendom. One who more than any other deserves to be classed among these writes: "Resignation to the will of God is the whole of piety. * * * Our resignation may be said to be perfect when we rest in his will as our end, as being itself most just and right and good. Neither is this at bottom anything more than faith, and honesty and fairness of mind; in a more enlarged sense, indeed, than these words are commonly used." [1]

Goethe, who studied and reflected on religious questions more than is generally supposed, saw that in such a disposition of mind lie the native and strongest elements of religion. In one of his conversations with Chancellor Müller, he observed: " Confidence and resignation, the sense of subjection to a higher will which rules the course of events but which we do not fully comprehend, are the fundamental principles of every better religion." [2]

By the side of two such remarkable men, I might place the opinion of a third not less eminent than they—Blaise Pascal. In one part of his writings he sets forth the " marks of a true religion." Sifted from its physical ingredients, the faith he defines is one which rests on love and submission to God, and a clear recognition of the nature of man.

Here I close these studies on the Religious Sentiment. They show it to be a late and probably a final development of mind. The intellect first reaches entire self-conciousness, the emotions first attain perfection of purpose,

---

[1] *Fifteen Sermons* by Joseph Butler, Lord Bishop of Durham. Sermon " On the love of God."

[2] *Unterhaltungen*, p. 131.

when guided by its highest manifestation. Man's history seems largely to have been a series of efforts to give it satisfaction. This will be possible only when he rises to a practical appreciation of the identity of truth, love and life.

INDICES.

I. AUTHORS QUOTED.

Allen, H., 208.
Anaxagoras, 106.
Arnold, M., 249, 271.
Aristotle, 105.
Augustine, St., 20, 57, 93, 128, 191, 194, 274.
Bain, A., 9, 25, 52, 59, 87, 91, 244.
Barlow, H. C., 201.
Baxter, Richard, 60.
Boehmer, H., 7.
Boole, Geo., 24, 44, 104, 105, 108, 111.
Bunsen, 109, 251.
Butler, Bishop, 60, 119, 276.
Carlyle, 243.
Catlow, J. P., 14, 64.
Chateaubriand, 250.
Comte, A., 11, 39, 128, 187, 194, 252.
Condorcet, 267.
Cory, J. P., 191.
Coulange, 245.
Creuzer, 90, 106, 119, 127, 200, 212, 222.
Cussans, 210.
Dante, 93.
Darwin, C., 71, 88.
Dick, 266.
Dickson, J. T., 73.
Etheridge, J. W., 190.
Ferguson, 66.
Ferrier, J. F., 20, 28, 43, 97.
Feuchtersleben, 8, 54, 73.
Feuerbach, 194.
Fothergill, J. M., 61.
Gibbon, 264.

Goethe, 277.
Gurney, J. J., 119.
Hall, Bishop, 50, 77.
Hamilton, Sir W., 24, 29, 91, 95, 99, 256.
Helmholtz, 11, 14, 18, 22.
Hegel, 29, 88.
Herbert of Cherbury, 149, 260.
Hobbes, 81.
Hodgson, S. N., 104, 126, 128, 134.
Holtzmann, A., 259.
Humboldt, A. von, 92.
Humboldt, W. von, 6, 53, 67, 93, 112, 113, 214, 246, 252.
Hume, David, 81, 187, 219.
Hunter, John, 9.
Jacobi, 88.
Jevons, W. S., 25, 204.
Kant, I., 25, 29, 32, 49, 91, 105, 194.
Kolk, Schroeder van der, 72.
Kitto, 74.
Koppen, 37, 214.
Law, Wm., 49, 87, 263, 272.
Laycock, 75, 245.
Lessing, 56, 254.
Lewes, 187.
Liddon, H. L., 129, 250.
Mansel, 87, 88.
Maudsley, H., 9, 150.
Mill, J. S., 18, 87, 91, 97, 223.
Mohammed, 71, 75, 114, 256.
Morell, J. D., 88.
Morley, J., 223.
Müller, 130.

Müller, Max, *preface.*
Naville, E., 256, 263.
Neander, A., 241.
Novalis, 41, 43, 107, 124, 243.
Oersted, 103.
Oken, L., 7, 186.
Paget, J., 63.
Parker, Theo., 88.
Pascal, 56.
Plath, 129.
Rousseau, J. J., 118.
Saussure, Necker de, 220.
Schlagintweit, E., 187.
Schleiermacher, 88, 275.
Schoolcraft, 63, 146.
Schopenhauer, A., 11, 13, 51, 82, 91, 269.
Schwarz, 207.

Senancourt de, 53, 180.
Spinoza, 9, 14, 17, 41, 42, 51, 98, 104.
Spencer, Herbert, 29, 39, 98, 104, 236, 260.
Swedenborg, 75.
Steinthal, 101, 246.
Tertullian, 211.
Theophilus, 191.
Thompson, 31.
Todhunter, 25.
Tyndall, 87, 132, 255.
Voltaire, 249.
Westropp, 62.
Wigan, A. L., 76.
Williams, J., 76.
Wordsworth, 41, 42, 180.
Windelband, Dr., 101, 102, 108.

II. SUBJECTS.

Absolute, the, 102, 106.
        consciousness of, 161.
Adam, as prophet of the moon, 170.
Adjita, 178.
Adonis, 165.
Aeon, 165, 166.
Agdistis, an epicene deity, 65.
Ahura-Mazda, 113, 166, 184.
Allah, 230.
Amitabha, 175, 185.
Analytic propositions, 32.
Androgynous deities, 66.
Animism, 163.
Anointed, the, 176.
Anya-Mainyus, 166, 184.
Anthropomorphism, 193.
Antinomies, of Kant, 29.
Aphrodite, 65, 241.
Apocalypse, the, 171.
Apollo, 67, 241.
Apperception, 156.
Apprehension, 142.
Arab idea of time, 165.
Argumentum de appetitu, 231.
Aronhiate, a Huron deity, 221.
Arrenothele deities, 66.
Art, religious, in Orient, 15; in Greece, 16; Christian, 209, 241; useless and immoral, 241.
Assyria, flood myth of, 169.
Athanasius, his doctrine of the Trinity, 191.

Atonement, doctrine of, 222.
Avalokitesvara, 214.
Aztecs, 80.
Baghavad Gita, the, 189.
Babylon, rites of, 74.
Baldur, 176.
Baptism, 138, 226.
Beauty, the line of, 15, 211.
      the religion of, 241, 244, 245.
Belief, its kinds, 141.
Brahma, 65, 169.
Brahmans, highest bliss of, 57; doctrines, 168, 169.
Breidablick, 176.
Brutes, religious feeling in, 88.
Buddha, 37, 57, 80, 120, 146, 156, 261, 271.
Buddhism, four truths of, 13; theories of prayer, 121, 150, 214; last day, 169; myths, 175, 176; monotheism of, 187, 247, 256.
Bull, as a symbol, 204.
Cabala, Jehova in, 65.
Canting arms, 212.
Cause, not a reason, 38; in physical science, 91.
Celibacy, Romish, 61.
Cerebration, unconscious, 149.
Chance, the idea of, 93.
Chinese character for prayer, 129.
Christ, see Jesus.

Christianity, doctrines of, 190, 257, 264, 274; symbol of, 203.
Christmas tree, the, 215.
Cockatrice, the, 77.
Commonwealth, ideal of, 247.
Consciousness, forms of, 17, 20.
Confucius, doctrine, 122, sq.
Continuity, law of, 11, 16; principle of, 95.
Contradiction, law of, 27, 102.
Correspondences, doctrine of, 217.
Cosmical relations of man, 112, 268.
Cotytto, 65.
Cow, as a symbol, 204.
Craoshanç, 176.
Creation, myth of, 166.
Crescent, a phallic symbol, 62.
Cross, a phallic symbol, 62; as phonetic symbol, 210; variants of, 210.
Cult, the, 199 sq.
Culture, religion of, 243, 244, 253.
Cybele, 65; priests of, 66, 219.
Dactyli, the, 184.
Darkness, terror of, 185.
Day of Judgment, the, 172.
Deity, see God.
Design, argument from, 110.
Desire, meaning of, 53.
Deus, 185; triformis, 191.
Deva, 185.
Didactic rites, 225.
Divination and prayer, 137.
Dramatic rites, 226.
Dual law of thought, 27, 102; division of the gods, 182, 183.
Edda, mythology of, 175, 215.
Eden, garden of, 175.
Ego, the, 19.
Egoism of religion, 272.
Egyptians, doctrines of, 80, 222; prayers, 115; pyramids, 212; lotus of, 214.
Emotions, origin of, 10; exclude thought, 19; in religion, 49; of fear and hope, 50, 51; esthetic, 14.
Entheasm, 148.
Epochs of nature, 164 sq.
Epicene deities, 66.
Epilepsy and religious delusions, 75.
Eros, 72.
Esculapius, emblem of, 200.
Esthetic emotions, 14, 244.

Ethics, grounds of, 266.
Excluded middle, law of, 27, sqq.
Expectant attention, 74, 129.
Explanation, limits of, 38.
Faith in religion, 107.
Fascination, 74.
Fear, in religion, 50, sqq.
Female principle in religion, 62, 183.
Feridun, garden of, 175.
Flood, myth of, 169, sq.
Fingers, as gods, 184.
Force, orders of, 133.
Freedom, 105.
Friends, sect of, see Quakers.
Future life, doctrine of, 250, sq.
Gallican confession, the, 138.
Generative function in religion, 62, 72, 73.
Genius as inspiration, 149.
Gnosis, the genuine, 74.
Gnostic doctrines, 166.
God, as father, 70; spouses of, 69, 71; mother of, 68; sexless, 71; earliest notions of, 78; incomprehensible, 98; throne of, 167; love of, 73, 263, 276.
Gods, hierarchy of, 181; quantification of the, 186; of lightning, 207.
Good, final victory of, 179.
Grasshoppers, prayers against, 131.
Greeks, art of, 16; doctrines of, 80; sophists, 96.
Gudmund, King, 175.
Hades, 186.
Hare, the Great, 212.
Hell, 186, 258, 274.
Hercules, 72.
Hermaphrodite deities, 66.
Hesperides, the, 175.
Hierarchy of the gods, 181.
High places, worship of, 215, 216.
Historic ideas, 232.
Holy spirit, as inspiring, 138; brooding, 167.
Hope, in religion, 51 sqq.
Horæ, the, 165.
Humanity, the religion of, 194, 253.
Ignorance, in relation to religion, 82.
Illumination, 140.
Immortality, doctrine of, 255.
Indians, American, 125, 157.
Insanity, religious, 76.

Inspiration, 137.
Intelligence, one in kind, 96; as the first cause, 106, 111.
Irmin, pillars of, 213.
Ischomachus, prayer of, 126.
Israelites, the Messiah of, 176.
Janus, an epicene deity, 65.
Jehovah, 65, 156.
Jemschid, king, 175.
Jesus, face of, 67, 241; conception of, 71; wounds of, 130; wisdom of, 144; as second Noah, 170; teachings, 178, 260; prayer to, 187; execution of, 203; death of, 222.
Judaism, 187.
Judgment, day of, 172.
Kalpa, of Brahmans, 168.
Knowledge, forms of, 21.
Kosmos, the, 72, 144, 167.
Lateau, Louise, 130.
Law, defined, 40; of excluded middle, 27; oldest, 248.
Laws, the, of thought, 26, sq.; 101, sq.; not restrictive, 105; as purposive, 108.
Light, as object of worship, 183.
Lightning, the, in symbolic art, 207.
Life, the perfect, 57.
Lingam, the, 66.
Lingayets, sect of, 66.
Logic, applied, 23; abstract or formal, 24; mathematical, 24; laws of, 101, sq.
Logos, the, 42, 106.
Lotus, as symbol, 213, sq.
Love, as religious emotion, defined, 58, 60, 262; of sex, 61, 63; law of, 73; of God, 73, 263, 276.
Ma, a goddess, 183.
Maitreya, 170.
Mamona, a Haitian deity, 68.
Märchen, the, defined, 157.
Marriage condemned, 69.
Maypole, as a symbol, 215.
Melitta, 65.
Memory, physical basis of, 10; ancestral, 73.
Memorial, rites, 225.
Messiah, the, 176.
Millennium, the, 173, 268.
Michabo, an Algonkin deity, 183.
Mind, growth of, 7; extent of, 8, 271; as seat of law, 163.

Miracles, 110, 130.
Mithras, 65.
Mohammed, notion of god, 71; inspired, 146.
Mohammedanism, 187, 224.
Monotheism, origin of, 80, 81; 186, sq.
Moral government of the world, 112.
Morality, independent of religion, dualism of deities, 182, 249, 266, 267.
Mormonism, 61.
Motion, first law of, 11; relation to time and space, 35; manifestations of, 77.
Myth, the, defined, 156.
Names, sacred, 156.
Natural selection, in sensation, 10; in logic, 101.
Nature, meaning of, 4, 39, 105; epochs of, 164.
Nemqueteba, 240.
Neo-Hegelian doctrine, 194.
Nirvana, the, 13, 57, 257.
Noah, 170.
Nous, the, 106.
Oannes, 170.
Obelisk as symbol, 215.
Odainsakr, 175.
O lin, 53, 259.
Optimism, 112, 269.
Order, in things, 90, sq.
Osiris, 165.
Pain, defined, 17.
Parsees, doctrine of, 80, 166, 184.
Pantheism, 188, 194, 247.
Papas, a Phrygian god, 183.
Paradise, lost and regained, myths of, 173, sq; future, 257.
Pentalpha, the, 212.
Perfected commonwealth, idea of, 247.
Perfected individual, idea of, 239.
Personal survival, idea of, 255.
Pessimism, 11, 112, 269.
Persians, ancient, 176.
Personality, the, 19, 270.
Phallus, worship of, 62, 66, 214, 216.
Phanes, the orphic principle, 190.
Philosophy of religion, defined, 3; of mythology, 159; of history, 232.
Phrygian divinities, 183.
Pillar worship, 215.
Pleasure, defined, 14.
Polarization, as a principle of thought, 183.

Porte Royale, miracles of, 131.
Postulates of religion, 80.
Prayer, 117, sq.
Progression of development, 109.
Protestantism, 128, 130, 250.
Protogonus, 167.
Psyche, and love, 72.
Pythagoras, his thoughts on number, 189.
Quakers, sect of, 76, 115, 138, 147.
Quantification of the predicate, 22; of the gods, 186.
Quetzalcoatl, 212.
Reason in religion, 106, 107; drawn from sight, 186.
Rebus in symbolism, 212.
Regin, as name of gods, 90.
Relative, the, 106.
Religion, science of, 3; philosophy of, 3; personal factor of, 81; not concerned with phenomena, 110.
Reproductive function in religion, 62.
Res per accidens, 182.
Resignation, doctrine of, 128, 135.
Revelation, marks of, 140.
Rig Veda, the, 125.
Rite, the, 217, seq.
Roland, pillars of, 215.
Roman Catholics, 76, 138, 141, 187, 250.
Sabians, myths of, 170.
Sacraments, 227.
Sacrifice, idea in, 218; vicarious, 222.
Saga, the, defined, 157.
Saint Brigida, 146.
Saint Gertrude of Nivelles, 146.
Sakyamuni, *see* Buddha.
Saturnian Era, the, 175.
Science of Religion, 3; as knowledge of system, 92; of mythology, 158.
Secularization of symbols, 204.
Sensation, defined, 9; excludes thought, 19; of pain and pleasure, 10.
Sentiment, the religious, 3; emotional elements of, 79; rational postulates of, 87; religion of, 250.
Serpent, as emblem and symbol, 200, 206, 207.
Sev, an Egyptian deity, 165.
Sex, love of, 61, 63; in nature, 71, 72, 216.
Shekinah, the, 66.

Siddartha, a name of Buddha, 121.
Similars, law of, 204.
Sin, sense of, 225.
Sight, as the light-sense, 186.
Siva, worship of, 66, 214.
Soul, the, 19, 271.
Specific performance in rites, 218, sq.
Stigmata, the, 130.
Sufficient reason, principle of, 91.
Sukhavati, 175.
Supernatural, defined, 4; its relation to symbols, 203.
Swedenborg, 75, 217.
Symbol, the phonetic, 200; origin of, 202; related and coincident, 203.
Symbolism, defined, 200.
Synthesis of contraries, 37.
Synthetic propositions, 32.
Tathagata, a name of Buddha, 121.
Tau, the Egyptian, 210.
Theology, 4.
Thor, hammer of, 210, 239.
Thought, as a function, 17; laws of, 26, 101, sq.; as purposive, 108.
Tien, Mongolian deity, 185, 216.
Time, not a force, 11; but believed to be one, 165.
Tlapallan, 175.
Tree worship, 215.
Triads, the Celtic, 190; Platonic, 191.
Triangle, the equilateral, 212.
Trinity, the doctrine of, 191; symbol of, 212.
Triplicate relation of numbers, 190.
Tritheism, of Christianity, 190.
Truth, what is, 21; eternal, 41; as answer to prayer, 137.
Tulan, 175.
Unconditioned, the, 29, 34, 37, 98, 100.
Uniformity of sequence, as cause, 91, 92.
Unknowable, the, 29, 34, 99, 100.
Valkyria, the, 53.
Valhalla, 250.
Varuna, an Aryan god, 125.
Vendidad, the, 175.
Venereal sense, the, 64.
Vicarious sacrifice, theory of, 222.
Virginity, sacredness of, 69.
Virgin Mother, the, 68.
Volition, *see* Will.
Voluspa, the, 171.
Wabose, Catherine, 146.

Water, as the primitive substance, 167.
Will, the, 16; of God, 38, 42; as a cause, 90.
Wish, the religious, 52; definition of, 79.
World, moral government of, 112; creation and changes, 164; light of the, 185.

Xisuthrus, 170.
Year, the Great, 169.
Yima, reign of, 175.
Ynglyngasaga, the, 218.
Yocauna, a Haitian deity, 68.
Zarathustra, 80, 114.
Zeruana akerana, 166.
Zweckgesetze, 108.

BRINTON'S (D. G.) WORKS. The Myths of the New World. A Treatise on the Symbolism and Mythology of the Red Race of America. Second edition, large 12mo, $2.50. Large-paper (first) edition. $6.00.

"The philosophical spirit in which it is written is deserving of unstinted praise, and justifies the belief that in whatever Dr. Brinton may in future contribute to the literature of Comparative Mythology, he will continue to reflect credit upon himself and his country."—*N. A. Review.*

The Religious Sentiment, its Source and Aim. A contribution to the science and philosophy of religion. Large 12mo. $2.50. (*Just ready.*)

CONWAY'S (M. D.) Sacred Anthology. 8vo. $4.00.

"He deserves our hearty thanks for the trouble he has taken in collecting these gems, and stringing them together for the use of those who have no access to the originals, and we trust that his book will arouse a more general interest in a long-neglected and even despised branch of literature, the Sacred Books of the East."—*Prof.* MAX MULLER.

DEUTSCH'S (E.) LITERARY REMAINS. With a Brief Memoir. 8vo. $4.00.

CONTENTS:—The Talmud—Islam—Egypt, Ancient and Modern—Hermes Trismegistus—Judeo-Arabic Metaphysics—Semitic Palæography—Renan's "Les Apôtres"—Worship of Baalim in Israel—The Œcumenical Council—Apostolicæ Sedes?—Roman Passion Drama—Semitic Languages—Samaritan Pentateuch—The Targums—Book of Jashar—Arabic Poetry.

"A noble monument of study and erudition."—*N. Y. Tribune.*

GOULD'S (REV. S. B.) LEGENDS of the PATRIARCHS AND PROPHETS. Crown 8vo. $2.00.

"There are few Bible readers who have not at some time wished for just such a volume."—*Congregationalist.*

HAWEIS' (REV. H. R.) THOUGHTS FOR THE TIMES. Sermons by the author of "Music and Morals." 12mo. $1.50.

"They have a special interest as exhibiting the treatment which old-fashioned orthodoxy is just now undergoing at the hands of the liberal clergy.—*Pall Mall Gazette.*

MARTINEAU'S (JAMES) WORKS.

Essays, Theological and Philosophical. 2 vols. 8vo. $5.00.

Mr. Martineau's contributions to the *Prospective, Westminster, National,* and other Reviews attracted the attention of the best minds in both England and America, and produced a marked and favorable impression upon men of all denominations.

The New Affinities of Faith. 12mo, paper. 25 cents.

STRAUSS' (D. F.) THE OLD FAITH AND THE NEW. 12mo. $2.00.

"Will make its mark upon the time, not so much as an attack upon what we venerate as an apology for those who honestly differ from the majority of their brothers."—*Atlantic Monthly.*

TYLOR'S (E. B.) PRIMITIVE CULTURE: Researches into the Development of Mythology, Philosophy, Religion, Art, and Custom. 2 vols., 8vo. $5.00.

"One of the most remarkable and interesting books of the present day. . . . It takes up man . . . at the remotest periods of which we have any knowledge, and traces his intellectual growth . . . from that time forth. . . Admirably written, often with great humor, and at times with eloquence, and never with a dull line. . . . The many students of Darwin and Spencer in this country cannot do better than to supplement the books of those writers by . . . these really delightful volumes."—*Atlantic Monthly.*

"One of the few erudite treatises which are at once truly great and thoroughly entertaining."—*North American Review.*

PUBLISHED BY HENRY HOLT & CO.

AUSTIN'S (JOHN) JURISPRUDENCE. Lectures on Jurisprudence, the Philosophy of Positive Law. By the late John Austin, of the Inner Temple, Barrister-at-Law. Abridged from the larger work for the use of students. By ROBERT CAMPBELL, 1 vol. 8vo. $3.00.

MAINE'S (SIR HENRY SUMNER) WORKS. Ancient Law: Its Connection with the Early History of Society, and its Relation to Modern Ideas. By HENRY SUMNER MAINE. 8vo. $3.50.

"History read from the point of Law, and Law studied by the light of History. It is consequently a book that addresses itself as much to the general student as to the lawyer."—*Westminster Review.*

"Mr. Maine's profound work on Ancient Law in its relation to modern ideas."—*John Stuart Mill.*

"Sir Henry Maine's great work on Ancient Law."—*Nation.*

"A text-book for all English students of jurisprudence."—*Saturday Review.*

Lectures on the Early History of Institutions. 8vo. $3.50.

"In the power of tracing analogies between different institutions, in the capacity for seeing the bearing of obscure and neglected facts, he surpasses any living writer."—*Nation.*

Village Communities and Miscellanies. (*In preparation.*)

MILL'S (JOHN STUART) MISCELLANEOUS WORKS. Uniform Library edition. 8vo. Tinted and laid paper, $2.50 per volume (except volume on Comte). The 12 volumes in a box, $29.00; half calf or half morocco, $59.00.

 Three Essays on Religion. 1 vol.
 The Autobiography. 1 vol.
 Dissertations and Discussions. 5 vols.
 Considerations on Representative Government. 1 vol.
 Examination of Sir William Hamilton's Philosophy. 2 vols.
 On Liberty: The Subjection of Women. Both in 1 vol.
 Comte's Positive Philosophy. 1 vol. $1.50.

CHEAP EDITIONS.

 The Subjection of Women. 12mo. $1.25.
 Principles of Political Economy. 12mo. $2.50.
 Memorial Volume. John Stuart Mill: His Life and Works.
Twelve Sketches, as follows: (His Life, by J. R. Fox Bourne; His Career in the India House, by W. T. Thornton; His Moral Character, by Herbert Spencer; His Botanical Studies, by Henry Turner; His Place as a Critic, by W. Minto; His Work in Philosophy, by J. H. Levy; His Studies in Morals and Jurisprudence, by W. A. Hunter; His Work in Political Economy, by J. E. Cairnes; His Influence at the Universities, by Henry Fawcett; His Influence as a Practical Politician, by Mrs. Fawcett; His Relation to Positivism, by Frederick Harrison; His Position as a Philosopher, by W. A. Hunter. 16mo. $1.00.

STEPHEN'S (J. F.) LIBERTY, EQUALITY, FRATERNITY. Large 12mo. $2.00.
A criticism of "Mill on Liberty."

"One of the most thorough overhaulings of the moral, religious, and political bases of society which they have recently received. . . . . Everybody who wants to see all the recent attempts to set things right analyzed by a master-hand, and in English which stirs the blood, will have a great treat in reading him."—*Nation.*

"One of the most valuable contributions to political philosophy which have been published in recent times."—*London Saturday Review.*

PUBLISHED BY HENRY HOLT & CO.

ADAMS' (PROF. C. K.) DEMOCRACY AND MONARCHY IN FRANCE, from the Inception of the Great Revolution to the Overthrow of the Second Empire. By Prof. C. K. Adams, of the University of Michigan. Large 12mo. Cloth. $2.50.

"A valuable example of the scientific mode of dealing with political problems."—*Nation.*

"Full of shrewd and suggestive criticism, and few readers will peruse it without gaining new ideas on the subject."—*London Saturday Review.*

"Remarkably lucid writing."—*London Academy.*

CHESNEY'S (C. C.) MILITARY BIOGRAPHY. Essays in Military Biography. By CHARLES CORNWALLIS CHESNEY, Colonel in the British Army, Lieutenant-Colonel in the Royal Engineers. Large 12mo. $2.50.

"Very able."—*Nation.*

"Uncommonly entertaining and instructive."—*N. Y. Evening Post.*

"Full of interest, not only to the professional soldier, but to the general reader."—*Boston Globe.*

FAMILY RECORD ALBUM. In Blanks classified on a New System. Large quarto, gilt edges, 328 pages. Cloth, $5. Half Morocco, $8. Full Morocco, $15. Levant or Russia, $25.

THIS BOOK for keeping family records has been made because the editor felt the need of it and supposed that many others felt the same need.

The pages are of eight kinds, called respectively Family, Genealogical, Tabular, Biographical Heirloom, Domestic Economy, Travel, and Miscellaneous.

FREEMAN'S (EDWARD A.) HISTORICAL COURSE. A series of historical works on a plan entirely different from that of any before published for the general reader or educational purposes. It embodies the results of the latest scholarship in comparative philology, mythology, and the philosophy of history. Uniform volumes. 16mo.

    1. **General Sketch of History.** By EDWARD A. FREEMAN, D.C.L. 16mo. $1.25.
    2. **History of England.** By Miss EDITH THOMPSON. $1.00.
    3. **History of Scotland.** By MARGARET MACARTHUR. $1.00.
    4. **History of Italy.** By Rev. W. HUNT, M.A. $1.00.
    5. **History of Germany.** By JAMES SIME. $1.00.
    6. **History of the United States.** By J. A. DOYLE. With Maps by Francis A. Walker, Prof. in Yale College. $1.40.
    7. **History of France.** By Rev. J. R. GREEN. (*In preparation.*)
    8. **History of Greece.** By J. ANNAN BRYCE. (*In preparation.*)

"Useful not only for school study, but for the library."—*Boston Advertiser.*

SUMNER'S (PROF. W. G.) HISTORY OF AMERICAN CURRENCY. With Chapters on the English Bank Restriction and Austrian Paper Money. To which is appended "The Bullion Report." Large 12mo. With diagrams. $3.00.

"The historical information which it contains has never been brought together before within the compass of a single work."—*N. Y. Tribune.*

"A most valuable collection of facts, thoroughly digested and properly arranged. . . . Has a freshness and vivacity rarely found in works of the kind."—*Atlantic Monthly.*

www.ingramcontent.com/pod-product-compliance
Lightning Source LLC
Chambersburg PA
CBHW032056220426
43664CB00008B/1030